ART & INSPIRATIONS

Judith Baker Montano

C&T PUBLISHING

Copyright © 1997 Judith Baker Montano

Developmental Editor: Barbara Konzak Kuhn

Technical Editor: Diana Roberts

Cover Design: Rose Sheifer, Graphic Productions

Cover: Original artwork, *Victorian Pansies*, by Judith Baker Montano

Book Design: Rose Sheifer, Graphic Productions

Watercolor Illustration: Judith Baker Montano

Photography by Judith Baker Montano unlesss otherwise noted.

Library of Congress Cataloging - in - Publication Data

Montano, Judith.

    Art and inspirations / Judith Baker Montano.

      p. cm.

    Includes bibliographical references and index.

    ISBN 1-57120-038-X (hardcover). —ISBN 1-57120-037-1 (pbk.)

    1. Silk ribbon embroidery. 2. Patchwork. 3. Crazy quilts. 4. Montano, Judith. I. Title.

TT778.S64M64 1997

746.44—dc21   97-14715

                                           CIP

Kanagawa is a registered trademark of the Kanagawa Company.

Mokuba is a registered trademark of Mokuba Co., Ltd.

Nymo is a registered trademark of Belding Heminway, Inc.

Ott-Lite is a registered trademark of Environmental Design Concepts, Inc.

Ultrasuede is a registered trademark of Springs Industries, Inc.

Published by C&T Publishing

P.O. Box 1456

Lafayette, California 94549

Printed in Hong Kong

10 9 8 7 6 5 4 3 2 1

Photo: Bill O'Connor

To Ernest Russell Shealy...
my husband, my lover,
my friend

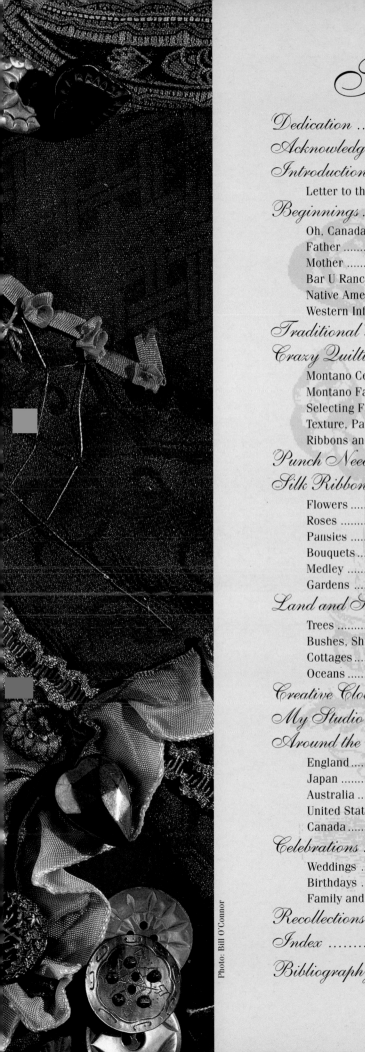

Photo: Bill O'Connor

Table of Contents

Acknowledgments

Writing a book of any kind is time consuming and very much like giving birth. You work for hours on end: creating, writing, sketching, photographing, editing, designing, and marketing. Weeks and months race by, deadlines are always looming, and with one great final effort the book is born! All this major effort is worked around family duties, traveling, teaching, and correspondence; but, when you are on the road as much as I am, it is a harrowing experience for me and those who work with me. I am fortunate to have the support of many people—my family, the Hensley family of C&T Publishing, my editor Barb Kuhn, technical editor Diana Roberts, and designer Rose Sheifer.

I wish to acknowledge Madeleine and Jason Montano, my beloved children, who have given me years of support, encouragement, and unconditional love. I look at them as my greatest creation for they are confident, creative, and interesting people.

My family has enlarged in the last two years as I have married, becoming the stepmother of three wonderful women, Kristin, Dana, and Tara, and grandmother to four bright and beautiful children, Nicole, Rie, Gen, and Kelse. I have a new sister-in-law, Wanda,

In memory of Alan Carter ...

but she and I are really sisters! I now have three interesting sons-in-law, Jim, Eric, and Yo; four brothers-in-law, Stanley, Paul, Lawson, and Carl; many nieces, nephews, and the list goes on and on. I love my new family because they accept me for just being me and have welcomed me with open arms.

My family in Canada, my parents Joyce and Allen Baker, my brother, Jim Baker and my sisters, Karen, Joy, Gloria, Kathy, and Christina…my godparents, Harry and Muriel Hays, and all my honorary aunties and uncles who helped

raise me…I thank them all for the years of support; without them I would not be who I am today.

I have been surrounded with strong women friends all my life and I could not have survived without them…

Thank you to Carol Moderi, Maren Francis, Pat Rogers, Anne Riseborough, Ruth Stoneley, Judith Wright, Di Pettigrew, Gloria McKinnon, Sherry Elder, Eva Yagino, Faye Walker, Frances Lange, Ora Harlan, Carmalita Davis, Lee Lock, Carol Hays Alberstat, Niona Case, Sandra Marsh, Frances Dover, Kathy Getchius-Sorenson, Joan Smokosky, Bessie Trembley, Holly Van Kleek, Rachel Walters, Shisiko Ono, Lola Meagher, Helen Weinman, Babz Seawell, Alice Hays, Alexandra Lober, Dorothy and Gracie Lefthand, Grandma Baker, Grandma Shantz, Eva Yagino, Yakako Onoyama, and Marla Miles.

There have also been a number of good men in my life whether for lessons to be learned or for lifetime friendship…

I wish to acknowledge Frederick Montano, George Elder, Grandpa Baker, Charlie Kennedy, Tino Cantu, Johnny Hodges, George Whitney, Bill Johnson, Takeo Maejima, Michael Redshirt, William Lober, Bill Lober Jr., Dr. Chris Bigland, Dan Hays, Grandpa Bacca, Jake Evans, Grandpa Bigland, George French, Don McKinnon, Alan Carter, Stuart Lange, Tom Walker, Claude Cruise, Gary Nyberg, Don Orthner, Peter Wella, and Chief Mark Lefthand.

And, I am a very fortunate woman in that I have found the love of my life at the age of fifty. Ernest Russell Shealy is the center of my life, and my world has a special glow to it since he became my husband.

Introduction

Letter to the Reader

Thank you dear reader and student, without you there would be no books, videos, card lines, honors, or career. Many of you have become friends over the years and many of you have gotten to know me through my work.

A retrospect is a layout of a lifetime of work or a period of one's life. It is an honor to be asked to produce a retrospect of one's work, but I was a bit hesitant to start because my life is a careful balancing act between the public Judith Baker Montano and the private Jude Shealy. Many readers have followed my progress over the years, watching my children grow up in the photographs and reading "between the lines." I often receive letters from people who have picked up on my personal life, just by reading my books. Because I try to write my books in a way a friend would talk to another over a cup of coffee, I suppose a few personal feelings have slipped in.

After much soul searching, I decided to go ahead with this book and to lay it all out for the reader to take in. My artwork and life experiences have made me the individual I am today, and when I look at the photographs that span fifty-two years of life, ten years of writing, eighteen years of quilting and needlework...I am amazed at the progress I have made!

Photo: Alan Carter

8

My artwork has truly changed over the years, not only because of techniques learned but because of skills developed and just living life. We should all keep a photo journal of our work and be forced to review it every year or so. It is a shock to see how much our artwork and skills evolve and improve. All those layers of life just make it better and better. How I wish I could keep all my experiences and skills gathered by age fifty-two and go back to my twenties! Not because I don't like being older, I adore my age and wouldn't want to change a thing about my life, but because I would be able to acknowledge my talents, accept them graciously, and produce a great more fiber art than I have. I realize that I still have many years in which to leave a body of work, but sometimes I regret the lack of confidence and wasted time bothering with all the petty bits that clutter our lives.

I hope you enjoy this book, it is laid it out in sections for your enjoyment. This book is meant to give you inspiration, to jog your memories, to enjoy as a visual feast. I want you to find something new in it everytime you pick it up, and hopefully you will find inspiration in the photographs of my work, my life, and travels. It has been an incredible journey, and when I saw the pages compiled, it suddenly made me realize what an unusual and full life I have had—all due to the love of expression with fabric, needle, and thread.

To all of you who have shared my life, from the people in the needlework and quilting world to those of you in my private life, I thank you.

Best Wishes
Judith

Beginnings . . .

Oh Canada

The Canadian Rocky Mountains are majestic and beautiful, and for me they are home. Whenever I hear people talk about the mountains of Colorado, the Blue Mountains of Australia, the French Alps or any mountainous area, I have to bite my tongue to keep from interrupting, for never have I seen anything quite so beautiful as my beloved Canadian Rocky Mountains! The Alberta foothills lay in the embrace of these majestic beauties and once you have lived in this area, no matter where you roam or for how long, this glorious region will, like the sirens, call you back.

I happen to be Canadian by the lucky chance that all my great grandparents immigrated to Canada in the early nineteen hundreds. They came from Europe, via the United States, hearts filled with hope, heads filled with dreams, hands and backs already work weary but willing to do more.

I am a mix of German, Scots, Cherokee Indian, French, Dutch and English, making it terribly confusing when filling out paperwork pertaining to race, color, and creed. I simply check all the boxes as a personal protest! I do not believe in categorizing people and we should all be treated as equals.

Father

My paternal grandfather, James Allen Baker, was born the youngest of seven sons in Coffeyville, Kansas. When it became apparent his chances for a career on the family farm would never materialize, he borrowed $75.00 from the Libertyville Bank and set off for Alberta, Canada. Settling in the Cayley farming district he soon had a job working with the haying crews. Within a few months he was able to pay off his debt.

My dad with a herd stallion

Aunt Lola and my father, Allen Baker

While filling out a money order at the local post office, he met my grandmother, Bessie Burns, who had come in for the mail. After a short courtship, my grandparents decided to marry and took the train to Calgary for the ceremony. Upon their return, the farming neighborhood all turned up at the train station to celebrate, along with the local character—an old Scotsman—who showed up in full regalia with bagpipes blazing.

Grandpa and Grandma Baker with my dad and Lola

My father, Allen Baker, was born in 1921 and gained a reputation early on, being quite a hellion and delighting in lots of pranks. Dad's greatest goal in life was to be expelled from school and his wish was finally granted in grade eight, after falling through the ceiling onto the teacher's desk. He had been hiding up there, all settled in with a candle and deck of cards, in order to miss the exams.

Luckily, my grandparents had instilled their son with a good work ethic and he was a smart businessman. From the time he was expelled Dad started collecting pigs and Hereford cattle, buying and selling till he could afford to buy a farm in the High River area. He rode a bus to Decatur, Indiana in order to go to auctioneer school, and from there he built up a huge cattle and farm auctioneering business. Allen Baker became a success, but he was still a hellion.

Grandma and Grandpa Baker

FAMILY MEMORIES

At last! A way to preserve old photographs in an economical manner. The antique photographs are photocopied, and the photocopy is used to transfer the picture to fabric. Commemorate your family photos using a variety of methods. I transfer images to fabric using the heat transfer method and the Australian turpentine method.

Grandpa Baker

Mother

Granddad Van Winkle, a Dutchman who worked most of his life as a train engineer, was part of the High River volunteer fire brigade. During one cold winter night they were called out to fight a fire. Four days later he was dead from pneumonia! My grandma, Adeline, was left penniless with three children to raise. She was extremely brave and took matters into her own hands. Keeping the youngest son at home, she sent my mother to Calgary to finish her schooling at a convent, and the oldest son went into the Royal Canadian Navy. Grandma hustled about playing honky tonk piano at night, cleaning hotel rooms during the day, and leading the church choir on Sunday. She has always been one of my heroes…she was a survivor!

My mother, Joyce Van Winkle, graduated from the convent and got a job as a telephone operator in High River. This job did not last very long as she met my father (via the telephone) and after a whirlwind courtship they announced their marriage plans. She was only seventeen years old and my father was twenty-four. They were married in the summer of 1944 and I was born nine months later, March 17, 1945, along with the spring calf crop!

I was fortunate to inherit my father's work ethic and my mother's artistic bent. No matter what else happened or what they did wrong or right as parents, these are gifts that I will always love them for and it is up to me to use these gifts wisely.

Fortunately, my mother is a multi-talented woman, excelling at needlework, pottery, music, and art. She employed her skills to keep us children busy and amused, and she taught me needlework at an early age.

Mom and Dad on their wedding day

My mother (age 18) and me

Uncle Don and
Grandpa Van
Winkle

Chester Van Winkle,
my grandfather

Grandma Adeline
Kruger Van Winkle
Shantz and me

Photo: Bill O'Connor

LIVING HISTORY

Our stitches reveal our influences and our environment. When a woman sits down to work on her stitching, she is not thinking, "Here in my hands lies my contribution to history…my link with the past and future." But give it some thought. Pieces of a prom dress, an aunt's silk handkerchief, a section of Uncle Bill's favorite vest: all are cut and arranged in a pleasing design to show the sentimental pieces. From a mother's gift to a family treasure, sharing your life through a bit of stitching creates a romantic token that becomes your family's history.

My mother Joyce, with Uncle Don and Uncle Dick

"ADOPTING" RELATIVES

Blood is not always thicker than water and we are sometimes faced with the dilemma of not liking some of our relatives or vise versa, or perhaps our family tree is not very colorful. I solved this problem years ago by adopting relatives via antique and second-hand shops.

I constantly search through old photographs and it breaks my heart to see all those faces, lost and in limbo with no one to care. I wish I could afford to take them all home. With my vivid imagination I could give each and everyone an interesting history! So I carefully choose my new relatives, give them names and an outrageous background. They find a place on the walls, in picture frames, and nestle in my photo collages…safe and well loved. Slowly over the years the lines of reality and fantasy have blended to create my unusual family.

FABRIC PAINTING

I discovered that acrylic paints could be diluted to water-color consistency and used to color the photographs on fabric. Simply dilute the paint (colors of your choice) and lightly color in the fabric photo areas. Allow the colors to blend into each other to give a watercolor effect. A second and third wash will give a deeper color.

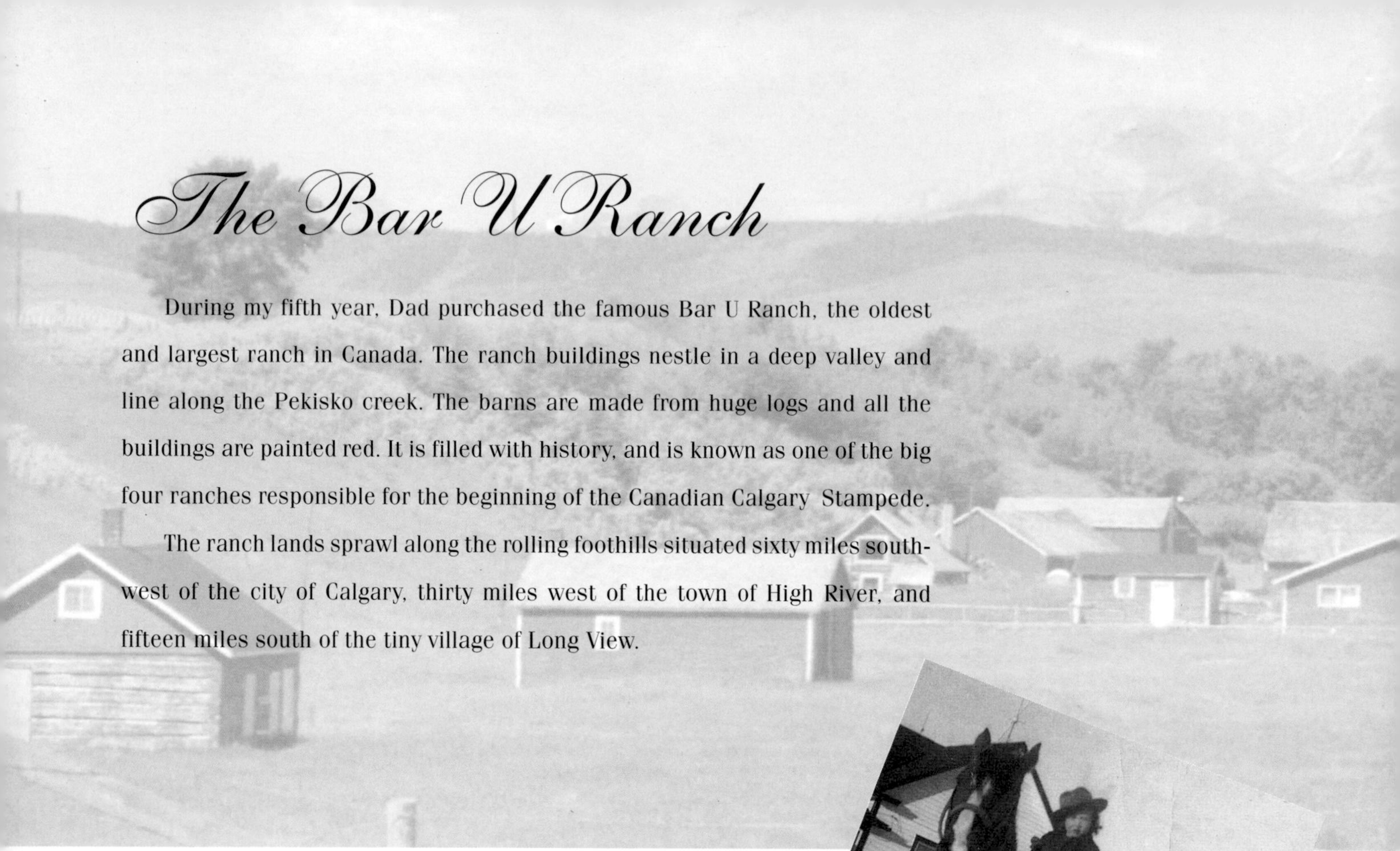

The Bar U Ranch

During my fifth year, Dad purchased the famous Bar U Ranch, the oldest and largest ranch in Canada. The ranch buildings nestle in a deep valley and line along the Pekisko creek. The barns are made from huge logs and all the buildings are painted red. It is filled with history, and is known as one of the big four ranches responsible for the beginning of the Canadian Calgary Stampede.

The ranch lands sprawl along the rolling foothills situated sixty miles southwest of the city of Calgary, thirty miles west of the town of High River, and fifteen miles south of the tiny village of Long View.

Today these buildings and surrounding acreage represent all Canadian ranching in the form of a federal living museum known as the Bar U National Historic Center.

*Judith (age 4)
and Dusty*

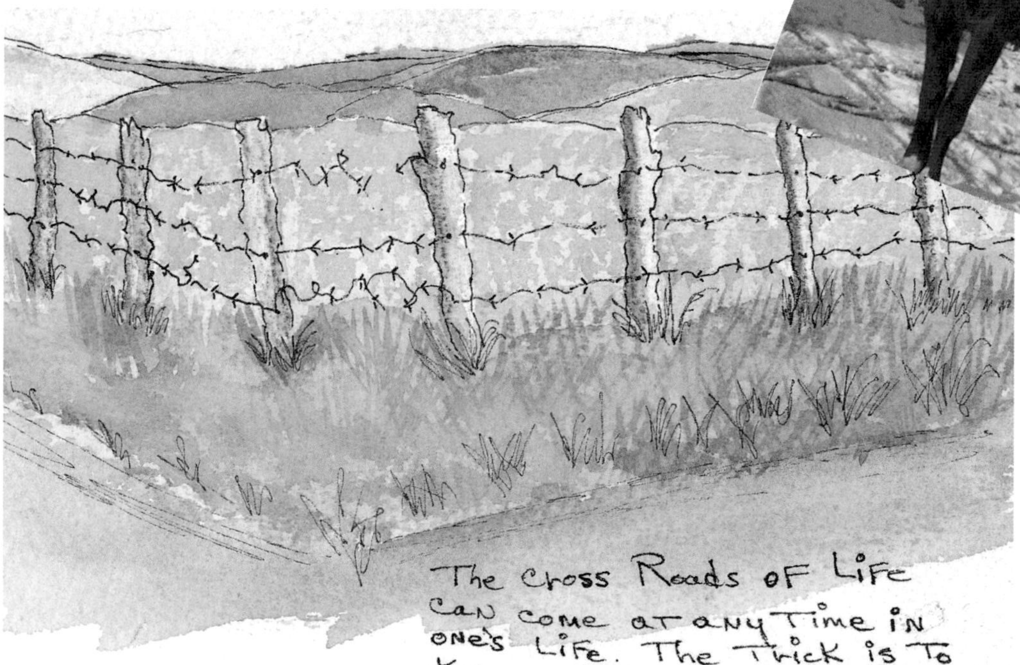

*The Cross Roads of Life
Can come at any Time in
one's Life. The Trick is To
Know when and what To do
about it!
Judith.*

*I loved the freedom
of the open land and
went every where on
my faithful old Dusty.*

On the ranch, I had two secret places that I favored mainly to draw and sketch in my many notebooks. I guess in looking back on it I was born an artist because as a tiny child a blank page and a fistful of crayons were my favorite toys. Later, when I could read and write, I would make up poetry and stories which I illustrated with pencil and ink drawings. I never shared them with people and kept them hidden under a big rock up on the side of a hill. Dusty, my pony, was quite happy to graze while I worked on my sketches.

Fred and Jason Montano with Bar U horses.

To achieve the casual look of country life, use homespun, checks, plaids, wool suiting, cotton calicoes, and lightweight denims. Keep the fabrics in medium intensities (dusty) to give an antique, faded aura.

Native American Influence

I had very few friends during my early years, so I was particularly happy when Dad hired Webster Lefthand, a Stoney Indian chief, to be the ranch foreman. Webster and his wife Dorothy had a big family and their daughter Gracie was around my age. I was fascinated with Gracie because of her exotic good looks and the fact that she could wear anything she wanted. She was a wonderful rider and we would spend many happy hours together. My favorite time was late summer when the Saskatoon berries ripened. We would ride up into the hills, find a good patch of Saskatoon bushes, then ride into the middle, drop our reins to let the horses graze, and eat berries till we could burst.

Dorothy Lefthand was very good at beadwork and I would spend hours watching her work on the leather jackets and gloves she was famous for. Sometimes she would let me help her and my love for beads started with Dorothy. I always felt at home with these people and to this day I go out of my way to visit whenever I return to my beloved Alberta.

From my Stoney Indian friends, I developed a love for rich, vivid colors and beads.

Beads are a passion of mine, and I use them as much as possible. They can accent Victorian stitches, ribbon embroidery, and punch needle designs. I often use them in place of French knots or to highlight a patterned fabric. Beads add shimmer, sheen, and that final sparkle! Good beads come in a wide variety of shapes, sizes, colors, and finish. For crazy quilting, keep beads in the 10 to 13 range. I use an average size 11 bead. A good rule of thumb is to use a needle size about one number higher than the bead size. Even so, I use a 10 sharps to sew on individual 11 beads and have little trouble with the beads sliding through. Many people use silk or cotton thread, but after years of wear and tear, it will break down. I recommend Nymo® thread for beadwork. Try a variety of beads in different shapes, colors, and sizes to add interest to your stitches.

Keeper of the Sacred Shield

Years later I discovered my Indian heritage and that my Great Grandmother Burns was part Cherokee. Her family thought it was something to be ashamed of, to be kept secret. It was a relief for me to discover my Indian roots because I have always felt different from others. My Indian heritage is a great source of pride for me and this is expressed in a lot of my artwork.

Photos: Bill O'Connor

Imelda DeGraw, the curator of textiles at the Denver Art Museum invited me to hold a one-woman show along with a display of antique crazy quilts. On the opening day, my dear Great Aunt Ora was busy telling her friends about her niece's work. She kept coming up to the art garment Keeper of the Sacred Shield and touching the garment that sent off an alarm. When the guard came over to tell her to keep her hands away from the display, she drew herself up to all four feet ten inches and looked him right in the eyes. She said, "Young man, my niece made this garment, so I can touch it any time I want!" After three reprimands and the threat of eviction, I had to walk her around the show, holding her hand to prevent anymore problems. Feisty old ladies are the greatest, and I hope I will be able to do her proud as I go along in life!

By using a variety of cords in the braided strap, you'll get a much more interesting tassel. Decorate the tassel with beads and aluminum Indian dance concs to give a jingle effect.

Made for the West Point Pepperell Challenge "Old Glory, Long May She Wave," presented by Margaret Peters. The author created this piece to depict her personal story, which includes images from the artist Thomas E. Mails.

Photo: Bill O'Connor

25

Western Influence

I have many stories to tell about my childhood, but one constant was my artwork. It was terribly important to me and a way of expressing myself. I have always been fascinated with people who had the guts to follow their dreams and to be artists. When I was a little girl on the Bar U Ranch, I had several sources of inspiration. The first of these was Bert Smith, a bachelor artist who lived in Long View. His specialty was mountain scenes done in oils. He would travel far into the mountains with pack horses and spend several weeks creating sketches and photos for future paintings.

Bert had one endearing quality: he loved children and wanted all of them to be artists. If we went to visit Bert, he would give us each a blank journal and encourage us to draw in it. He always kept the journals at his place, encouraging us to visit often and once we filled up the journal, he would pay us a quarter! He would let us watch him as he worked on his big canvases and over the years he became a well-known Alberta artist.

After a serious riding accident, Bert returned to his artwork, but the ability to paint a large canvas evaded him, so he turned to pen and ink sketches and photography. Bert still resides in Long View and he is working on a third generation of art students. My children, now twenty-one and twenty-four, remember him fondly. On their summer visits to the ranch, they took art lessons from Bert, earning a Canadian quarter and many dear memories.

Photo: Bill O'Connor

Madeleine Montano (age 20)

Judith, Johnny Hodges, and Madeleine Montano.
When I was a little girl I was introduced to Johnny Hodges. I was told he was a pen and ink artist, and he showed me some of his work, which I loved. But more than that I was amazed that he would be interested in what a kid had to say…that's just how Johnny is, he has friends of all ages.

Charlie Beil was a famous Canadian cowboy artist, and a great friend of Charlie Russell. Together they worked in Montana and Alberta during the great roundup days. They were both painters and sculptors, each gaining international fame. I got to know Mr. Beil during my summer job at the Banff Springs Hotel. One free day I walked up to his house and introduced myself. We had a wonderful afternoon together and Mrs. Beil kept us plied with hot tea and lots of cookies. With that one visit we became fast friends and after looking at some of my sketches, he agreed to give me art lessons. I learned so much from Mr. Beil and I look back on this summer as a big turning point in my life. I started using pen and ink for my sketches and went so far as to sell some through the local saddle shop in High River. (This is where I met Johnny Hodges, a local artist who worked making beautiful saddles.)

Judith and brother, Jim Baker

Arapaho West *is an Indian-inspired garment, highlighted with crazy quilting, ribbons, and punch needle embroidery.*

Judith (age 21)

On my last day with Charlie Beil, he drew a sketch of two saddle horses tied to a hitching post and signed it "to my friend Judie Baker... love, Charlie Beil."

Duncan Crockford was a world-renowned oil painter and his favorite subjects were the rolling Alberta foothills and the Rocky Mountains. He came from eastern Canada, and after spending a summer in the Kananaskas area, he settled in Calgary. Commissioned by my father to paint the Bar U foothills, he and his wife Wyn soon became fast family friends. Never was there such a character! Duncan was very fond of the grog and Wyn made it her life-long duty to keep him on the straight and narrow. It was a thankless job to say the least. He was a marvelous oil painter and his canvases were very popular throughout Canada, and thanks to Wyn's vigilance he produced a great number of paintings. He encouraged me to be an artist and to ignore my parents fears that all artists were starving to death in a garret. "Why look at me," Duncan would bellow, "I am a perfect specimen of the successful artist...don't listen to all the nay sayers lassie, follow your heart."

When I married at the age of twenty-five, Duncan promised me a painting of the ranch buildings.

Photo: Bill O'Connor

29

This Cowgirl is a Lady, *made for the Superstar Fashion Show, presented by Fairfield Processing Corp. and Concord Fabrics.*

My future husband stopped by to visit the Crockfords the day before the wedding and was shown the painting. After several toasts they headed for the pub and all was lost. Duncan showed up at our wedding in kilt and full regalia, minus the painting. Somehow it was lost at the pub. His gift to us was a piper who piped us down the aisle and Duncan's rendition of the Highland Fling.

Years later Dad gave me a Duncan Crockford painting of Goathead Mountain and it hangs in my living room. Every time I look at it, I fondly remember the mad Scotsman who encouraged me to follow my dreams and danced at my

Photo: Brad Stanton

My Mentor

My one year at Trinidad Junior College in Colorado was one of the big turning points in my life. My sister and I traveled to Colorado on our Great Aunt Ora's recommendation. She had told me the journalism program was an excellent one and I should enroll. After settling in the dorm, I set out to the journalism department, only to find the course consisted of working for the school newspaper. So, I quietly enrolled in a few art courses and my life took a dramatic turn because I met my mentor there. The art department was run by one man, Bill Johnson, and it was mutual admiration from the first meeting. Bill is a big, gruff man who is terrified that anyone should discover his soft heart. He is blessed with a witty sense of humor just short of being cynical. In his early days, he was an illustrator for the "Saturday Evening Post". After my first book was published, my family and I stopped to see him in Trinidad while on holiday. Upon looking at the book he said, "Well, Baker, you got married and you had kids, and you're fat, but by God you are using your talent and I'm proud of you."

Many people do not like crows, believing they represent death and bad luck. In Indian lore the crow is the messenger, who comes to call us home or to warn us of change.....

Long and short stitch black, purple, royal blue...

Metallic straight stitches....

The crow is my token bird..... No matter where I travel there are two crows to watch over me.... always two. I find crow feathers where ever I travel..... once in the lobby of the Hyatt Regency hotel!!

wedding in a kilt that twirled up and proved the old myth that Scotsmen do not wear underwear under their kilts!

As I think back to my childhood, I realize that my surroundings and the people who made up the community had a profound influence on me. The isolation of the rural Alberta countryside only helped to heighten my imagination and the profound beauty of the area sharpened my eye.

Judith with her cousin Faye and sister Karen

Traditional Beginnings

On Country Time *made for the Kaleidostar Fashion Show presented by Fairfield Processing Corp. and Concord Fabrics.*

When my son was born I decided that it was time to make him a quilt. The women on my father's side were all known for their beautiful needlework and quilts. My mother was also a wizard with any type of needlework and sewing, but somehow these talents held no interest for me until my son was born. I was a late bloomer and at the age of twenty-six, I finally began my love affair with needle and thread.

For practice sake, I first started a king-size Ohio Star quilt made from batik fabrics I purchased on a visit to Thailand. All I can say about this quilt is that it was very busy and rather ugly. Next I attempted appliqué animals on a single bed quilt. Because I was always looking for shortcuts, I decided to ap-pliqué and quilt at the same time...so with huge stab stitches, I appliquéd the animal shapes in place, went right through the batting and the backing, creating a puckery, uneven stitch. This too was rather ugly and never did get finished.

King-size quilt made by the author, adapted from a Blanche Young design.

My first award-winning quilt was a Blanche Young Trip-Around-the-World design which I split into four portions using a maple leaf design. It was a wedding gift for my baby sister and her husband. Before giving it to them I entered it in the Calgary Exhibition and Stampede and it won Best of Show—the same award my great grandmother, Lola Devore Burns, had won in 1934. It was a thrill to win this award and I gave my sister the ribbon along with the quilt.

In 1981, I decided to make a quilt depicting my Alberta ranch home and I drew up a design of the mountains as viewed from the living room window back home. With Canadian maple leaves and vines, I made a border that also featured the family cattle brands and the neighboring ranch brands.

Halfway through the making of this king-size quilt, I received the brutal news that my beloved godfather had died of a massive heart attack. The one man in my life who had loved me for myself was gone. It was too much for me to comprehend. After attending his funeral and helping my godmother with the reception and making sure she was well cared for, I returned to Houston, Texas, and quietly had a nervous breakdown. I could not accept the fact that he was gone. I was overcome with grief and regrets. One of my honorary aunties, Bessie Trembley, who lived in Switzerland, came to my rescue. This wonderful woman who was so busy with her own life, running a pension in the French Alps, flew to Houston and arrived at my doorstep like a fairy godmother. She took over the restaurant, antique shop, and my family, allowing me the time to grieve and to heal.

I am glad to have had the discipline of traditional quilting because it taught me many techniques and above all an appreciation for all the work that goes into making a fine quilt.

I am not the first woman nor the last to work out my grief with quilting, and there are countless stories out there. But I am grateful to Aunt Bessie because she helped me through a very sad time in my life. I am also grateful for my quilting, which helped me handle my sadness. Out of pain and grief comes creativity and healing, and that is why some artists create their greatest works from a broken heart...

I worked on my ranch quilt with the goal of completing it in my godfather's memory. I don't remember a lot but the soothing rhythm of the hand quilting helped me come to grips with the loss of this wonderful man. In this quilt a thousand tears of sorrow are stitched along with a thousand joyful memories.

This quilt went on to win Best of Show at the 1982 Texas State Fair, winning over 380 Texans. It took Best of Show at the Calgary Exhibition and Stampede, Best of Show at the Pacific National Exhibition in Vancouver British Columbia, the Margaret Steel award and a Mountain Mist award. Last, but not least, it took second place honors at the Houston Quilt Show. My ranch quilt then retired to hang in my house for many years.

Later when Aunt Muriel died in 1993, I added her name to the ranch quilt and gave it to their son Dan in order to ease his great loss. Together we decided to give it to the Bar U Historical Center in the name of the Baker and Hays families. It was presented at the grand opening of the museum ranch site and it felt good to have it hang there for all to see, a testament of true love and undying gratitude to two people who accepted me as their daughter. I find it very soothing to know that my ranch quilt is snug and safe in the bosom of my beloved Alberta foothills.

Pekisko Memories

Crazy Quilting

Crazy quilting is a special love of mine, the answer to all my diverse pleasures. What other handcraft combines embroidery, sewing, appliqué, laces, ribbons, buttons, beading, painting, and color design? Crazy quilts have always fascinated me. Though other crafts may distract me, I am always drawn back to beautiful, outrageous crazy quilts. They remind me of mysterious, glittering jewels, like gypsy cousins peeking out from a patchwork of traditional sister quilts.

I believe one's background and upbringing preface our special interests. The texture of my background has a lot to do with my love for crazy quilting.

Crazy quilting is a part of my heritage, too, handed down from my grandmother. Several years ago, in a chest filled with handiwork of Grandmother Baker's, my aunt showed me a lovely crazy quilt tucked away with the tablecloths. It is a wonderful link with the past and my own passion for crazy quilting. The quilt is a spiritual bond between me and my grandmother.

Photo: Bill O'Connor

38

CRAZY QUILT METHOD

I like to work in the crazy quilt method, as it is the most "painterly" of all the quilting methods. You must think as an artist while working in this technique. The muslin base becomes your canvas. The chosen fabrics are the paints and there is no pattern—only your imagination is your guide. As there is no set pattern for crazy quilting, the outer perimeter of the muslin becomes a guideline, then the fabrics are laid down in a pleasing design. However, this layer of fabric is only the first layer of color. Various needlework techniques will be laid over the layers to create further visual interest.

Some of the fabrics in my grandmother's quilt are disintegrating, but it still has a story to tell. Past memories are woven into this quilt. It includes pieces of her dresses, material from my grandfather's best suit, and shirting from those he wore in the fields. One piece is from a baby dress that belonged to little Agnes, their first child who died at the age of five. A special handkerchief, brought back from the Great War by an uncle, is proudly displayed. The crazy quilt is not as lush or fancy as other crazy quilts, but it is just as much a document of history, a tribute to a young farm wife who labored to create something beautiful for her home.

My friends would tease me about my obsession with crazy quilting and I was willing to put up with this because I was so delighted to find a quilting and needlework technique that fed my artistic interests.

Judith (age 51)

Samuel Percival Pussycat, better known as Sam

Judith (age 21)

I highly recommend to my students that they keep a record of their work over the years. The easiest way is to take photographs and put them into a binder. You will be amazed at the improvement and the change in your designs. I keep both slides and photographs. My collection spans twenty years. I am very surprised to see how my work has changed and progressed over the years. In the beginning of my crazy quilt efforts, the piecing is quite large and the embroidery along the seam lines is the only decoration. Later I started adding beads, a little lace, and ribbons. As the years passed and I learned more techniques, my work has become more painterly and textured.

Detail of Crazy Quilt Friends

FRIENDSHIP QUILTS

The crazy quilt is a perfect vehicle for a group effort such as a friendship quilt. Forty friends in my Texas quilt guild contributed to a surprise going-away gift for me that kept me busy and happy assembling the donated pieces in my new home. We all shared the pleasure when it won Judges Choice at the Colorado State Fair. The ease of incorporating little pieces of special things, dates, and initials, and assembling assorted shapes and sizes of the contributions makes a crazy quilt an ideal project for guilds and church groups.

After seven years of living overseas, we moved to Houston, Texas, and I finally had the opportunity to enroll in a quilting class. There were eight of us and we became close friends. The teacher was well versed in traditional quilting. She kept us very busy making fourteen-inch pillow tops, with each week bringing about a more complicated pattern. This was during the late seventies and the fabrics were very limited in colors and prints, not like the beautiful selection we have today.

After making dozens of pillows, we decided to hold a bazaar, and it was so successful we started a quilting group. From this class of eight and our teacher, the Kingwood Quilt Guild was started. This is the only organization I ever stayed with as I am not much of a joiner and I have always walked to a different drummer. This group was very important to me and I learned so much not only in quilting but also in the give and take of committee work. I became the publicity chairman and later when we grew too big, I was president and had to set up a formal structure. Today the Kingwood Quilt Guild is a huge group that does a lot of good for their community, and the work they produce is staggering.

Because I had always been attracted to crazy quilting, I went to my teacher to inquire about the technique. Instead of saying she did not understand the method, she belittled the crazy quilt look and said I shouldn't bother with it. I took this to be a challenge and I was determined to master the method. I had a double-edged reason for wanting to learn this technique: it looked a great deal like the tissue collages I used to make in the seventies and I thought I could jazz up some of my clothes using this method in fabrics. Also, I was very tired of the rigidity of traditional quilting as it was taught to me. I was chafing at the bit for a more free-form technique. I felt quite inhibited with the rules of quarter-inch seams, points meeting, and cottons only. There were so many pretty fabrics out there and I was anxious to use them. The artist in me wanted out!

Finally, I decided to teach myself. If our forebears could make crazy quilts, so could I. Because I couldn't find how-to information and because crazy quilts were not popular then, I kept very quiet about it. The first piece I made was a sixteen-inch square which later became the cover for a small footstool. It was a pathetic effort but I rather enjoyed the process.

Crazy quilt appliqué was easy for me to do but the embroidery stitches were really difficult for me and very, very frustrating. It is nearly impossible for me to learn crafts from the written word, and I have to be shown in person or have lots of diagrams and pictures. So this first effort was uneven and unsatisfactory, making me wish I had paid more attention when my mother tried to teach me embroidery as a little girl. Thankfully the square wore out very fast and there is no evidence remaining of this first attempt at crazy quilting.

My next project was a vest made of old silk ties and this piece I keep as a lesson in humility! I painstakingly appliquéd the slinky pieces down but forgot to press as I went along...what a mess. The embroidery is still uneven and I used cotton floss, all six strands in places, and it is much too heavy. Also the threads blend into the fabrics and do not show up enough. I still have the vest and every once in a while I examine it and I am pleased to say that I have made progress over the years!

Now and Then

43

Montano Centerpiece Method

I kept practicing and trying to perfect the appliqué technique for crazy quilting, but it soon became evident to me that the best part of crazy quilting was the embellishments. After numerous attempts I finally came up with a method I call the Montano Centerpiece Method, a five-sided centerpiece method for piecing traditional crazy quilts. This hurried the base work because it is done entirely by sewing machine. Over the years this method has become associated with crazy quilting and many people think this is how the Victorian women applied their fabrics to the base fabric...but, I can assure you the centerpiece method was perfected by a dyslectic artist who came up with the idea with lots of trial and error.

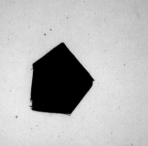  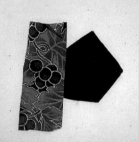

Using a dark solid fabric (so it will recede), cut a small piece with five angles. Don't bulls-eye the piece; instead, set it off to one side to create a better balance.

Cut a wide rectangle and lay it along angle 1, right sides together.

Sew from the top of angle 1 to the bottom. Flip the rectangle over to the right side, trim out from the seam, and press.

Cut a second wide rectangle and lay it along angle 2. If you are right handed, work clockwise and if you are left handed, work counter clockwise. Sew from the end of the Previous Piece of Fabric (think of it as PPF) to the end of the second angle. Now cut from behind, and press.

Continue working until the five angles of the centerpiece are covered. Note that on angle 5 the wide rectangle must extend over rectangle 1 and 4. (There are two PPFs.)

Now cut more angles from the pieces you have sewn down. Be severe: cut from edge to edge. Think squares, triangles, and pyramids. In this case I now have six angles. This number will vary depending on how the pieces are cut.

Choose an angle and proceed with the second wave of rectangles. Note the rectangle strip has been pieced to create the illusion of more pieces and more angles.

Continue adding pieces in a clockwise or counter clockwise direction. Keep a good balance of color, texture, pattern, and solids as you work. Remember to trim out and press as you go. Always cut new shapes and sizes after each go around.

When piecing a rectangle strip to get across a long run, use a variety of shapes, such as rectangles sewn to a square then sewn to two triangles.

Embellish the piece.

Montano Fan Method

I have also developed the Montano Fan Method for piecing any projects that are twelve inches and larger.

Cut a corner patch of solid color fabric with three inside angles. Place in either bottom corner, flush with the foundation fabric.

Starting on the left side cut a wide rectangle. Lay it along angle 1, right sides together. Sew from one end of angle 1 to the other, using a long basting stitch. Trim excess from the seam. Flip the rectangle piece, and press. Don't worry if a tail hangs out, it will be trimmed when the next rectangle piece is sewn.

Lay the second rectangle along angle 2 following the cut angle and covering the Previous Piece of Fabric. Think PPF! If not, you will create V and L shapes, which are difficult to fill in.

Add the third rectangle fabric along angle 3, covering the PPF. Trim away the excess, flip the piece to the right side, and press.

Now cut new angles. Cut edge to edge and be severe. You want to get away from rectangular strip piecing. So think squares, triangles, and pyramids. Make sure you have a variety of sizes and shapes.

Start on the right side and fill in the cut angles. (In this case there are three, but you could have four or five depending on the angles chosen.) Note that the second strip in the second go around is pieced together. This helps to keep the work from looking "stripy" and keeps the piecing in proportion to the project.

Once again, cut more angles and proceed to fill in, starting from the left side. (Hence the title, Fan Method). Always trim the outside pieces that hang out beyond the base fabric. This keeps the piecing in better proportion.

Note some of the rectangle strips have been pieced to create the illusion of more angles. Note that the third go around has been trimmed to five angles and the next go around will proceed from right to left.

Continue to fan back and forth, from left to right then right to left, until the foundation is completely filled. Always trim the excess fabric from the seams to keep the work from being bulky. Cut angles after each "wave," making sure you have a variety of shapes and sizes.

Embellish the piece.

Selecting
Fabrics

One of the best things about crazy quilting is the infinite variety of fabrics it can employ. Virtually anything, from velvets to cottons, from lace to drapery fabric, can find its way into crazy quilting.

Whereas solid fabrics are the foundation of crazy quilting, they can be mixed judiciously with patterns and textures. Solids are the base for embroidery, paintings, and other details.

Because crazy quilting uses relatively small pieces, half yard lengths will do. If a piece is a large

Collage made by the author for her friend Ruth Stoneley of Brisbane, Australia, which depicts Ruth's mother as a bride and Ruth as a little girl. The fabric was designed by Ruth using Australian wildflowers as a theme.

decorator print with lots of color and design, you might buy a yard or more. Neutral colors that you'll use often might be stored in longer lengths, too. Old ties are terrific for crazy quilting and they can be quite inexpensive. Since most are a jacquard weave, the reverse design is on the back and you get two designs for the price of one.

Texture, Patterns, and Solids

In crazy quilting, it is very important to have a balance of texture, patterns, and solids. If you have too many busy prints, the work becomes a blur of confusion and the fancy stitches don't show up. It is important to "bounce" printed pieces off solids or textured fabrics. This adds interest and shows the pattern to the best advantage. The same is true of textured fabrics. If your crazy quilt is made up only of textured fabrics, the fancy stitches get lost in the nap of some textures. For each fabric piece to harmonize with its neighbors, they must complement each other in color and type.

Texture fabrics include moiré, wool, nubby fabrics, tweed, and velvets. Prints include any fabric that has a pattern, from a pindot to a large decorator print.

Photo: Chris Patterson

IMPORTANT RULE

In traditional crazy quilting, I have one important rule: Never put pattern against pattern and always "bounce" patterns against solids and textures.

Ribbons and Lace

Selecting Ribbon

The variety of ribbon offered today, from satin to silk, from wire to organza, all add to the beauty of crazy quilting. Different widths of ribbon can be used in different ways. Wide ribbon can be sewn like a fabric piece into the base work. Medium and narrow ribbons can be appliquéd to add interest to the fabric piece. These are a nice canvas on which to highlight special embroidery stitches. Very narrow ribbon can be woven through lace or twisted and tacked down with French knots.

Metallic cording and printed ribbons add to the effects of color, pattern, and texture. They act as accents and do not need further embellishment.

Ribbon Seam Covers

Lay a ribbon directly over the seam line and appliqué down on both sides. On most ribbons, it is nice to decorate them with embroidery stitches. Use embroidery floss that contrasts with the ribbon.

Meandering Ribbons

Use silk ribbon to decorate a fabric piece or wander over several. This ribbon is usually 4mm wide and is very soft and pliable; it handles almost like bias. It is available in a wide range of colors, too. Use this ribbon to create interesting pattern over the base work. The ribbon can be tacked in place with beads or French knots. Space close together to prevent the ribbon from snagging.

French Wire Ribbon Ruffles

Use wire ribbon 1" to 1½" wide to make ruffles. Scrunch the ribbon up like an accordian. Pull out to the desired length and tack in place. Ruffles can be highlighted with French knots, beads, and buttons.

CLEANING ANTIQUE LACE

Old lace, doilies, and hankies are found at antique and second-hand shops, estate sales, and garage sales. However, many lovely old pieces are soiled and stained and must be cleaned carefully before they can be used.

Try washing stained lace by hand in a mild detergent. Wrap it in a towel and squeeze out excess water, then let the lace dry on green grass. Rinse thoroughly and try again if the stain still appears. The chlorophyll in the grass will help bleach out the stain. Diluted laundry bleach might work on tough stains, but it must be rinsed very thoroughly and the lace must be washed after bleaching.

If all efforts to clean a stain fail, try cutting away the stained parts, or just accept the stain as part of the antiquity of the piece. Or, let the stain dictate the look and tea-dye the entire piece to match.

Selecting Lace

Lace acts as an element of texture in crazy quilting. By laying lace or a doily over a deep, rich color, you add drama. Laces, old and new, can decorate seams or accent a dull fabric.

Use long, narrow pieces of lace to overlay the seams or meander and zigzag across the crazy quilting. They can be highlighted with ribbon or embroidery stitches. Add beads or buttons for sparkle. Keep lace embellishments in the same mood as the rest of the work. Be aware of whether your project is pastel, dusty, or jewel-toned.

Judith's grand-daughter, Nicole Szilagyi, models a gray velvet vest highlighted with punch needle embroidery.

Punch needle takes on the shape of tiger lilies and bleeding hearts. Modeled by Alexandra Lober.

Navajo Indian blouse with punch needle

Punch Needle Embroidery

Like any other technique, punch needle embroidery requires practice, but it does not take long to get the stitches small and even!

Punch needle embroidery is an old Russian technique that uses a special tiny needle threaded with embroidery floss or silk. The fabric is stretched, drum tight, in an embroidery hoop and the design is worked from the back. The result is a carpet of tiny loops that create the design on the right side with the look of thick plush. The loops can be sheared to give the design a velvety look. The finished embroidery is very durable and washable.

Punch needle embroidery can be used to highlight a pattern in a special fabric. If the design of the fabric shows through to the back, you can follow the lines to punch needle parts of the pattern. The beauty of this technique is that it's very fast and pretty. Any embroidery pattern can be used, even line drawings from coloring books and magazines.

Start with a simple design and a medium-sized needle that will take about three strands of floss. Make sure the fabric is drum tight in the embroidery hoop or the stitches will not hold. Remember that the design is punched from the back, so it will face the opposite way on the front of the fabric. Check that the design is facing in the proper direction! On my free-form scenes, I complete the piece right up to the embroidery and then punch in the grass and tree leaves through more than one layer of fabric.

Silk Ribbon

Embroidery

My crazy quilting was becoming quite an obsession and I was searching for new techniques to add interest and texture to my work. After a few years of teaching in Australia, I became very interested in silk ribbon embroidery. Although I had been traveling to Tokyo, Japan, for several years to work for Kanagawa Silk Company, and they were using me to endorse their products, I had not seen silk ribbon used for floral embroidery.

One year in Canberra, Australia, Jenny Bradford, who has written many books on the subject, came to my crazy quilt classes. We had a good visit and I told her I was very keen to learn the silk ribbon embroidery technique. No matter how we tried, we could not arrange a time for a lesson, so armed with one of her books and a fourteen-hour plane ride back to America, I tried to teach myself the various ribbon stitches.

Because I have a dyslexia problem of right and left, and also being very tired from the trip, I managed to come up with a few original stitches. As I started experimenting with the ribbons, I soon discovered that I could use it in the same way as the silk threads. I started stitching silk flowers all over my crazy quilt pieces and discovered that ribbon embroidery could be combined with punch needle embroidery and beading.

I prefer my silk ribbon embroidery to look like my flower arrangements…very full and colorful. The Australians, English, and New Zealanders work in a more open design with the flowers being absolutely perfect and very delicate. I am a renegade in this department, and because I am self taught, I probably make traditionally trained embroideresses and quilters quite nervous. I am not worried about the correct needle, just as long as it fits, or about the proper threads and ribbons. I go more for the effect than the proper way of doing things. Although, going back to my earlier point of breaking the rules…I could do it the proper way if I had to, but only if I had to!

Flowers

I have always been fascinated with gardens and especially flowers. Vegetable gardening for me has been a complete failure and after years of battling grasshoppers, weeds, and hail, I realized that my carrots were costing me about a dollar each and I could buy them in better condition and at a better price at the market. This gave me the excuse to turn my gardens over to flowers, flowering shrubs, and trees. If it doesn't flower, the plant is not allowed in my garden.

By living in both Colorado and California, I now have two gardens. Ernest, my husband, has been guarding his one little vegetable patch in Los Angeles, and is quite upset at the row of pansies that are marching down the center of his veggie patch. I've assured him they will add some color, and besides, people often eat pansies in salads! I prefer a cottage garden filled with perennials, all happily mingling with each other, and a few annuals for extra border color. I inherited a green thumb from my Grandma Shantz. The stories in the book *Recollections* are a mix of memories of both my grandmothers. The house belonged to Grandma Baker but the garden I describe was Shantzie's pride and joy. People would drive seventy miles from the city just to see her flower gardens. They were a jungle of riotous color, vines along the fences, with arbors of roses and pansies scattered about for an extra surprise. She did not worry about color, and simply grew what she loved. This influence stays with me and I still prefer to garden in that style. My flower arrangements are always big bouquets of mixed flowers.

JUDITH'S CURLED LEAF

Here is a little leaf that works up very easily, but it will come out if you pull too hard. I use it for projects that will not get a lot of wear and tear, yet I have used it on my clothing without any worries. To begin, come up through the fabric and flatten out the ribbon using the needle as a "scootcher" under the ribbon. Decide on the length of the leaf and with the needle tip, push the ribbon towards the base so it will curl up. Now pierce the ribbon in the center and pull the ribbon down until only a tiny curl remains on the top, then go on to make another leaf. The secret is to know when to stop or the curled leaf will become a short Japanese ribbon stitch.

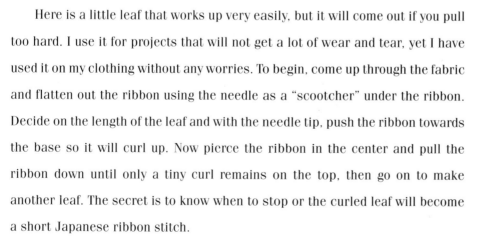

MONTANO SLOPPY KNOT

When I first started silk ribbon embroidery in 1986, I was not happy with the spaces left between my flowers. I wanted a more bunched look…so I started playing around with knots. I was able finally to produce a stitch that looks like a cascade of flowers, by using a variation of the French knot and using three shades or three complimentary colors of 4mm silk ribbon. Depending on the size of the flower, I start with seven wraps, then go back in the same hole. Letting the ribbon remain loose, I pull the ribbon through to the back. This makes a big loose knot. The next knot is wrapped six times, the next five, and so on, until you are down to one or two of three wrap knots, then just a few ones. Start again with another ribbon and intermingle the second knots in among the first. Add the third set of knots in the same manner, making sure to place the colors in a random fashion. If you wish to make a more delicate cascade, start with fewer wraps, such as four, three, two, or even one. I guarantee you that everyone will want to know how to do this stitch.

JAPANESE RIBBON STITCH

The Japanese ribbon stitch is an old stitch that has been used for years to represent saber-shaped leaves such as daffodils, tulips or iris. In the rush to get out there with teaching and books, many people have misrepresented this stitch and teach it wrong. To begin, come up from under the fabric and flatten out the ribbon. Decide on how long the leaf will be and pierce it at this length in the middle of the ribbon. Where the needle pierces the ribbon will be the tip of the leaf. Now pull the ribbon all the way through and do not leave a curled end (the ribbon will fold in on both sides of the leaf tip to make a saber end). This is the proper way to make this stitch and it is much more realistic-looking than the other variation, which has a curled end,

Roses

Roses are very romantic and for me they have been the symbol of love since time has been recorded. I like to use them in my collage pieces mainly because they add dimension to my work, and everybody in the world recognizes

the rose. They also come in a great abundance of color, size, and shape. In Alberta, Canada, the wild rose is our provincial flower and it grows profusely along the ditches, in the fields and scrub brush, and along the river banks. Whenever I see this beautiful, pink single rose with the yellow center, it takes me back in time and I'm laying in a field, listening to the drone of the bumble bees and the hum of the other insects while they dart about. Once in a while the insect serenade will be interrupted by the screech of a hawk or the bellow of a cow, reminding her calf not to stray too far. On a lazy day like that, I would stay for hours just watching those old fat bumble bees, their legs bulging with pollen, trying to memorize the shape of the roses. Later when I had a camera, the same number of hours would be wiled away trying to capture the bumble bee settled in a rose for that brief instant of rest they allow themselves.

Madeleine, the baby of our family, now twenty-one but still the baby, loves white roses and I always think of her when I see them. Much like a signature perfume, the white rose evokes memories of Maddy. I am sure that you also look at certain roses and think of someone. Why not use them in your needlework as a surrounding for a photo collage? Use them often as the theme of your project.

The climbing rose is an old-fashioned rose that adds grace and color to the garden. No cottage scene is complete without them. Sometimes I use the climbing rose to soften walls and fences or to add to an arbor. This adds an old-fashioned quality to your project faster than anything else I know. Roses can be fashioned from all types of materials and stitches, from the smallest little bud made from a colonial knot to a huge opulent wire-edged rose.

I am very fond of the concertina rose worked in satin or organza, as it makes up a full shape and my other flowers can be worked around them. The spider web rose, as well as the Bradford rose, work up into a nice shape. Also be aware of the buds and half open roses…these can be indicated by the rosette stitch and the rosette bud.

Pansies

It is fun to give personalities to flowers and we could never leave out the ever-cheerful pansy. It is the happy face of all the flowers, the one who greets you along the walkway. Sometimes I look out of my window during an early spring snow and there they are, smiling away as if it is a summer day. I suppose if I had to choose between all the flowers in my garden, I would choose the pansies. And if I had to narrow that down to only one variety, it would be the Jolly Joker pansy. It has my favorite color combination—purple and yellow-orange—and it also reminds me of special people who I have known.

Pansie Six-pack
Judith '96

Love is…
You with the gentle and happy nature
What makes you ask of me,
"What is this thing called love? and
Do you know what it can be?"

Surely my answer will not quench your thirst
For knowing more…
In my stumbling way, perhaps
I can tell you, but my way is poor

Love is a small and ill-treated word
When used deceivingly…it has no worth
But when love is used truthfully
It has all the beauty of heaven and earth

Photo: Chris Patterson

"Claude started me on my very first garden. It was just a three-foot square over here behind the pansies. I can still see it when I close my eyes. A jumble of Shasta daisies, a little patch of snapdragons, a single sunflower towering in the back, and these little purple and orange pansies in front. Claude gave them to me as a special gift from his garden. You know, they are called 'Jolly Jokers,' a truly appropriate name for such a cheerful little flower."

—excerpt from Recollections,
by Judith Baker Montano

Photos: Bill O'Connor

Bouquets

Because I like a heavy collaged look in my flower arrangement, I try to start with the heavy materials first, such as satin-sided ribbons, organza ribbons, and ombre ribbons. I make roses using the concertina method and place these in first. Everything else is built around these. At first they look very large but as you crowd them with other flower stitches and fill in with the Montano knot cascades, all of a sudden it takes on a full, opulent look. I try to save the leaves for last...something like saving the icing on the cake for last. By tucking under the flowers with leaves of lazy daisies, Japanese ribbon stitches, and Judith's curled leaf, I can come up with dozens of types of leaves.

The Victorians were very big on the language of flowers and bouquets often carried a secret message. I often visualize some poor soul admiring a beautiful bouquet whose message is "get lost and never darken my door again because I hate you!" Now by looking in my flower book that bouquet would consist of wild liquorice (I declare against you), basil (hatred), Saint John's Wort (animosity), cypress leaves (death), and sweet peas (departure); oh yes, and the sender could have added yellow carnations (disdain) and michaelmas daisy (farewell) just to make sure the reciever gets the message!

In looking through *The Language of Flowers*, I have found some of my garden plants carry a message for me…cape jasmine (transport of joy), for-get-me-not (true love), phlox (unanimity), canterbury bells (acknowledgment), morning glory (affection), coreopsis (always cheerful), hollyhock (ambition), peony (bashfulness), varigated tulip (beautiful eyes), day lily (coquetry), sweet pea (delicate pleasures… remind me to plant more of these!), blue violets (faithfulness), columbine (folly), white roses (I am worthy of you), lupine (imagination), ivy (marriage), and lemon tree (zest).

Medley

I think flowers should be categorized by personality as some of them remind me of people and moods. For example, the tea rose is rather elegant and above it all, and so is the Easter lily. These are rather stately grand dames and can alter the mood of the garden. I feel the same about tuber roses, delphiniums, and fox glove…all these beautiful flowers add a feeling of elegance to the garden. Then there are the exotic ladies…the ones who give the feeling of being slightly naughty and probably are…

The tiger lily is a great example and I always think of my storybook grandmother in *Recollections* who said, "He said that while I appeared to be a shy violet, I was really a tiger lily at heart! I wonder what he meant by that?" Her eyes twinkled mischievously as she smiled down at her granddaughter. Yes, I wonder, too.

The Bird of Paradise is another exotic lady and so is the Star Gazer lily. This magnificent hot pink and white bloom with its bright orange stamens is very exotic indeed and if you are not careful the orange pollen will stain everything it touches.

VARIEGATED RIBBONS

I like to use variegated ribbons whenever possible and sometimes make my own…I am aware that I will never get the same variegate twice. To make my own variegates, I use silk dyes, a watercolor brush, plastic sheeting, and five yards of silk ribbon in the lightest shade of my variegate. Perhaps the colors I have chosen are pale peach, lavender, and soft rose. I buy five yards of light peach and dilute my dyes down to dusty lavender and soft pink. Place the ribbon on the plastic. Using the watercolor brush, I touch the ribbon with lavender and rose, leave a space, and touch the ribbon again with lavender and rose. The colors will bleed nicely into each other.

The exotic beauties seem to be elusive as if you will never know everything about them. Some of the beautiful clematis blooms give off an exotic feel and so do the Australian lilies called Naked Ladies. The brilliant fuchsias fit into this category with their exotic pantaloons of color. The beautiful exotic opium poppy, bejeweled with glorious color and its insidious juices—the black center drawing in the victim—can really let your imagination run wild. I could go on and on.

Gardens

When you are working flowers into your projects with thread and ribbon, some flowers really make you think of people. Because flowers are so much like people, it never ceases to amaze me. One overly friendly flower is the cosmos and for some reason it never bothers me. Perhaps it is because they come only as a single plant appearing so bright and floaty; the fern-type leaves never seem to be offensive to its neighbor and they always brighten up the garden no matter where they land.

Lazy Daisy Stitch…will make wonderful daisies because a single stitch looks like a daisy petal. This stitch can also make good leaves for various plants. I have seen violets, daffodils, and tulips worked up in the lazy daisy.

Some flowers appear quite shy, and I always think of violets, lily-of-the-valley, and snow drops, who appear to be hiding their faces. Years ago I bought a wood violet plant and it has managed to spring up throughout my big perennial bed without anyone hardly noticing.

Some flowers appear rather friendly and inviting, like a good neighbor. The tall, yet charming hollyhock is one of my favorites. They remind me of an "open door, tea and cake on the porch" sort of friendliness.

The old-fashioned geranium is another friendly plant that evokes memories of grandmothers, cats curled up on the rocker, and the smell of home-baked bread. I never look at the bright red common geranium that I do not think of my Uncle Harry and my great Aunt Ora. Although they lived in different countries, Uncle Harry had a huge rambling house, and Aunt Ora had a small white-washed adobe

Remember that every variety of flower has a different green leaf or stem. This is very important and will make the difference between the ribbon flowers looking realistic and beautiful, or cheap and sleazy. So if you have daffodils, crocus, wattle, roses, and forget-me-nots, you will need five different greens and as many in threads if the stems will be showing.

Curved Whip Stitch…work this noodle shape into all types of fantasy flowers. I use them for cattails, orchids, gladiolas, or anything that is tall and exotic looking.

Montano Knot…this stitch makes wonderful cascading shapes as well as wisteria, delphiniums, fox glove, snap dragons, and hollyhocks.

Plume Stitch…use this free-form stitch to create astilbe and fern-type plants. It is also very good for grass shapes.

home. Harry planted beds of red geraniums, while Ora planted them in flower boxes on her porch. Either way the flowers said welcome to all the visitors that passed through their doors.

Some plants like petunias and marigolds can be just too cheerful for their own good, but I still line my garden borders with them. They act as the official greeters to my garden. Other flowers are just too friendly and become a real nuisance, sort of like a gossipy busybody. Nasturtiums are like that. You plant them and they stay in place for quite some time, looking charming and cheerful. Then, one day you turn around and there they are choking the life out of their neighbors. White Shasta daisies are just about as bad…they look so innocent and sweet, so you plant them on the right side of your garden. The following year they appear in the center and over to the left. The next year they have visited all the neighbors and joined hands! I just put up with these wandering busybodies and when it looks like they are about to take over the garden, I dig up the wanderers and give them to my neighbors and other interested gardeners.

Land and Seascapes

 **M**y crazy quilt landscapes have evolved over the years from stilted appliqué pictorials to free-form silk collages. My art training was in oil painting and I've always gravitated towards realism. Sometimes I work from photographs, but other times I create the "real" places I've fantasized about!

Many of my students want to create a childhood memory in their needlework and crazy patchwork. This poses a problem for them because they have to think like a painter instead of a needleworker or quilter. Instead of paint, they will use fabric, thread, and yarn, layering these much like a painter lays down layers of paint. The maker will also have to give some serious thought to the mood of the piece and what time of day it is, because this will effect the shadows and the light source. So many things to think about before they ever get started.

The first landscape made by the author; Yvonne Porcella taught the class where Judith learned the technique to burn silk edges.

New Mexico Will Always Get You

Each crazy quilt landscape begins with a sketch on paper. Photos or pictures, if used, should be clear and sharp (see Copyright Concerns, page 77). Try to simplify the shape of the land in your sketch. Remember, you can add details with embellishments. Once you are pleased with the sketch, transfer it to muslin and cut out adding a ½" (12 mm) all around. Early on, I struggled with the proportion from background to midground to foreground. I have been trained as a painter, and yet working with fabrics was difficult in the beginning because I was always forgetting that things in the background are far away in the

distance, and they will always be small with very tiny stitches and embellishments. The foreground is right in front where the viewer is standing, and it is in this area the needleworker will always put the most embellishment and detail.

So the stitcher must decide right away on the mood, time of day, the light source, and what lays in the background, midground, and the foreground. Next they must decide if this is to be a vertical or horizontal picture and the size of the finished project. Because the eye will always search for the horizon line, it is always good to decide on that right away.

Photo: Bill O'Connor

Painters use a few tricks to help the eye travel to the center of the painting. One rule is to never put the horizon line dead center in the picture. Instead, always make it above or below this line. By using the S shape (this could be the shape of a path, a winding stream, or a road that will travel from the foreground into the midground or background), you will draw the viewer's attention into the scene.

While all of this may sound terribly complicated just to produce one scene, it is the difference between a professional and realistic-looking project, or one that will always be in the workbasket. Please realize that the background, midground, and foreground may be indicated only by a few embroidery stitches or sketch lines, but they have to be there!

Another common mistake that we all make is trying to create a picture without building up the layers of color and detail. In other words, you must always think about what lies behind. For example, a tree needs roots to stand up straight. It also needs a trunk to support the large tree limbs, which support

I want to inform you about copyright law. I see copyright law being broken almost every day, and most of the time it is quite innocent; yet, other times it is a blatant infringement, with the culprit counting on the fact that litigation is expensive. There is a common courtesy of giving credit where credit is due. If you are using a published picture from a magazine or a gift card, you must never use the finished piece for commercial purposes. In other words, only if you are using it strictly for your own personal use, and then only once. You should get written permission if the finished piece is to be put on display. And if it is a method taught to you by another teacher, please credit them for the method. This is not only common courtesy, but also something that many people are ignoring. Be careful, and if you are ever in doubt, seek the advice of legal council.

the branches, which support the leaves and then the flowers. If you leave this process out, you create a "pigs-in-space" kind of look; it all looks floaty and disjointed.

Remember always that you are painting with fabrics. Look at the pattern sketch and determine the sequence for laying down the fabric pieces. The fabrics anchored into place are the foundation of the landscape scene. I stitch over every seam with embroidery stitches. The lines of the hills and mountains that edge up to the sky need a special treatment if they are to look realistic, so keep the embroidery on the side of the hills. Sometimes a simple running stitch is all you need. It can act as a drawing line to give detail.

Once all the seams have been decorated, I go over the piece with textural ribbon, such as silk or spark organdy. It can be twisted and manipulated, then held down with French knots or beads. Shadow and light are created by use of color, but you can increase shadow and detail with acrylic paints or permanent pens. Further texture and detail can be added with punch needle embroidery. But, take extra care as you are punching through two layers. Remember always that landscapes are creative impressions taking shape from your imagination and memories. You are the creator and the artist.

This might sound like a lot to remember, but after awhile it will become second nature to you. Even though I have a degree in art, it took me a few years to realize that the same applies to fabrics as it does to paints. You can see the progress I have made simply by looking at my work in *Crazy Quilt Odyssey, The Art of Silk Ribbon Embroidery,* and *Elegant Stitches* to realize the improvement.

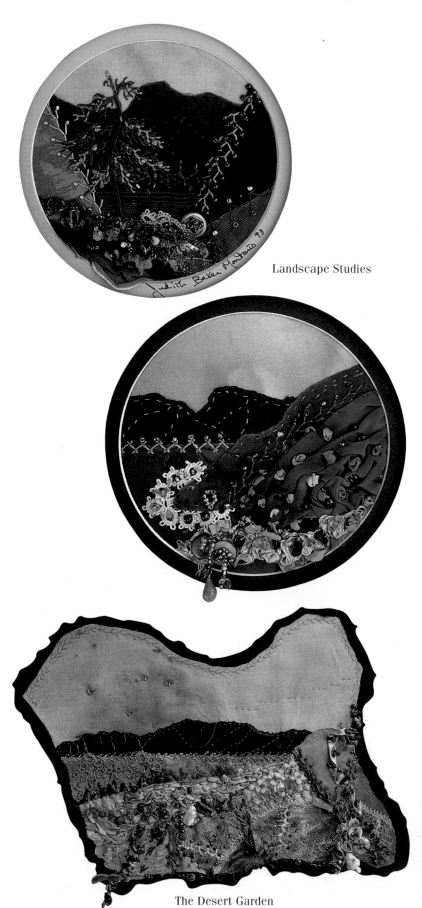

Landscape Studies

The Desert Garden

Recollections of Love, *made in memory of Muriel and Harry Hays*

 Trees

Trees are a never-ending source of fascination for me. They are such an essential part of the life cycle, and yet it seems mankind still hasn't grasped this concept. Trees bring us oxygen and shade. They give us shelter and food. In the ultimate sacrifice, they produce lumber for our practical and artistic endeavors.

When I was a little girl, I had a secret place high up on a hill about a mile fom the ranch buildings. It would take quite awhile to reach the top as it was very steep and rocky. My horse would have to zigzag back and forth as we climbed slowly towards the rocky outcropping near the top. Up there the rugged old bull pines grew, all gnarled and twisted with time. My mother was very fond of the huge pine cones they produced and I always brought some back for her. I would spend hours among the rocky ledges and the bull pines. In fact, I wrote a poem about them.

Up high where the bull pines grow
gnarled and wise with the passage of time
I'd sit in their branches and rock to and fro
with playmates of fantasy, pencils, and rhyme.
Oh, how I miss those old friends of mine!

These beautiful, yet rugged trees often show up in my creations. A good example of this would be the tree in the art garment Vision Quest (detail above). I have worked this tree in punch needle embroidery with many shades from gold to rust to darkest brown. The loops formed by the punch needle gives a rough texture, which suggests age and weathering. Floating behind the tree is the outline of an eagle, which suggests the vision quest, but also suggests the passing of time.

Detail of the art garment Vision Quest *shown on page 102*

The bull pines show up again in the Spirit Shield. This shield is made of deer skin, silk, silk threads, fetishes, and beads. My brother Jim gave me the deer skin as a gift. I used part of it to make an Indian baby carrier (pages 20-21) for our dad. When I started the Spirit Shield, I wanted something that would speak to me of my Alberta home and I instantly thought of the bull pines. After burning the edges of the silk to make the mountains and the hills, I surrounded the whole picture with one large bull pine. The way it bends and twines around the picture gives the illusion of depth. The fine punch needle detail of the tree is created by using a single strand of floss.

Whenever possible I take photographs of trees in order to build up a good reference file. At the same time, I am thinking about the materials I can use to create the tree trunk, branches, leaves, and flowers.

The tree in *Lady Lives On*, (on the front cover of *Crazy Quilt Odyssey*) is a mixture of stem and chain stitches, punch needle embroidery, and beads. By laying down rows of chain stitches and stem stitches, you can create drawing lines. Just remember that darks recede and lights come forward, so in order to give the illusion of the roundness of the trunk, start at the outside with the darkest color and work towards the middle, getting lighter and lighter. In this particular tree the pine needles are worked in punch needle embroidery with beads added for shimmer.

In Australia, the gum trees are absolutely glorious, outlining the horizon like graceful parachutes of leaves held suspended by undulating, twining branches. Some varieties have trunks mottled with patches of mauve, gray, and tan. This can be achieved in needlework with silk threads laid down in the satin stitch, or with short and long straight stitches. Just make sure the threads are smooth and silky. Some eucalyptus trees have long, stringy bark and this effect can be achieved with variegated yarns or with bouclé yarns couched with finer threads.

Detail of Lady Lives On

Always think of the texture of the tree trunk and what materials will give you the right look. This means you must keep a good supply of threads and yarns, from smooth to heavily textured, shiny to matte, fine to thick, single stranded to multi-stranded. Keep in mind that variegates can help you paint the project much easier than solid colors.

I often use the gum leaf shape for accessories, such as the Crystal Pouch. The pouch is made of Ultrasuede®, beads, and crystals. The edges of the leaves are burnt to give a dark edge. Next the leaves are overlapped and attached to the pouch.

Crystal Pouch

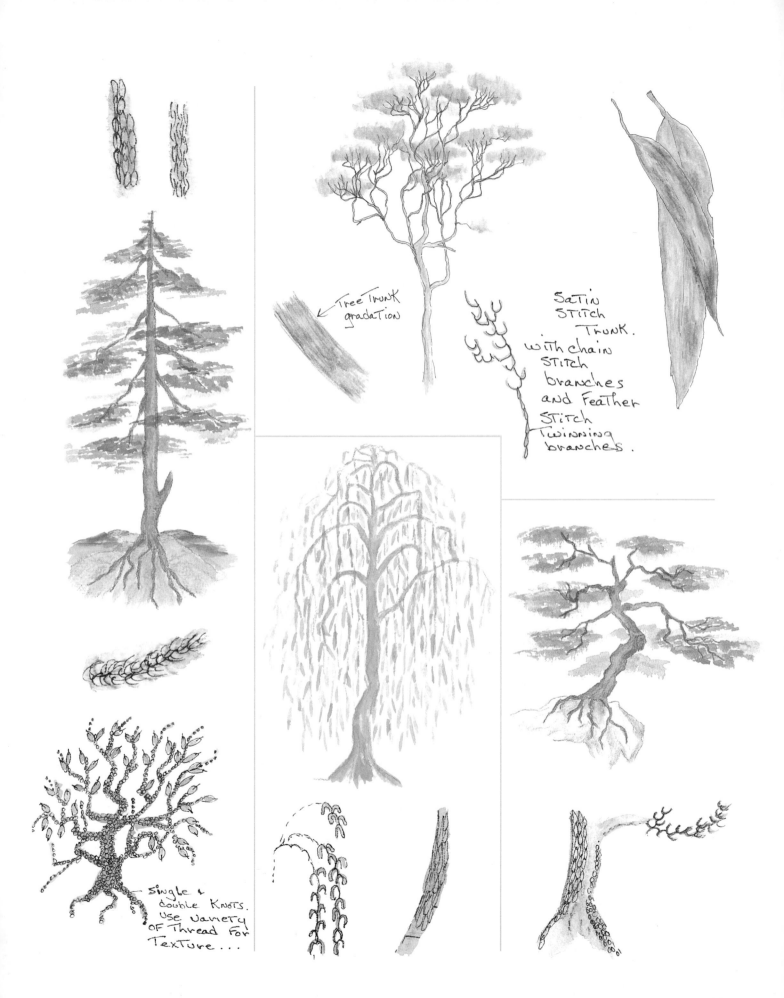

Tree Trunk gradation

Satin
Stitch
Trunk.
with chain
Stitch
branches
and Feather
Stitch
Twinning
branches.

Single &
double Knots.
Use variety
of Thread for
Texture...

Bushes, Shrubs, and Vines

What landscape, crazy patchwork, silk ribbon scene, or cottage piece would be complete without bushes, shrubs, or vines? We need these to indicate gardens and lawns in our work, or perhaps to add a touch of floral beauty to act as a highlight. Just remember the rule I gave you about building up from the background forward (page 72) and that the skeleton of the piece must be there. So before you add that climbing rose, there needs to be a wall or fence for it to climb on, and branches and leaves have to be there before you add flowers.

I like to distort traditional stitches in order to create greenery. Because I am totally self taught, I have come up with some very unusual stitches. I try very hard to learn the proper way to work the stitches before I distort them or push them into free-form embroidery. I like to use the example of Picasso, who was trained in formal art schools, breaking loose at a later date to create the Cubist style. The same applies to your stitches and embellishment techniques. Learn how to do them the right way, and to do them well—then have fun using them as a drawing and painting tool. Above all, do not be afraid to experiment and to use materials that you usually would not use. The only way you will find out if they work is to use them.

To create the look of a vine, often I will use a simple chain stitch. I can control the movement a bit better with this technique. One of my favorite methods is to use stranded silk and cottons that are on a tight twist. I unravel the strands and let them fall into place and then carefully couch them down with a matching thread. This is very time consuming, but the results are spectacular. They take on a very twisted and gnarled look. Nubby knitting yarns and chenille yarns can make excellent vines and roots. Just remember that these have to be couched down. If you have the opportunity to look at a cut bank or to see an eroded hillside, take note of the root systems exposed. They twist and branch just like the branches above ground and can make for very interesting texture studies.

COUCHED THREADS

There are so many beautiful threads and yarns out there to use in their entirety, and I often use these to indicate vines and underwater kelp or seaweed. By laying them in place, and couching them down, they take on a slinky, twining effect. Just remember that the finer threads will look furthest away and that the shade or tone of color will also create depth. A good example of this would be using fine metallic threads in the background, then three-ply silk in the midground and a mohair yarn for the foreground. Always keep depth and proportion in mind.

Outline and stem stitches can also make wonderful vines and by weaving these stitches over and under other shrubs, trunks, and branches, they take on a very realistic look. Always give it some thought as to what lays on top and what goes under. On cliffs and rock outcropping the roots are more interesting than the trunk and branches, so give this some thought when you are anchoring the tree or shrub to the hillside or cliff.

Vines that grow up walls and picket fences can be rendered in the feather stitch along with the outline stitch and the chain stitch. Just keep in mind where the base begins and work that in the heavier stitch. Use the feather stitch to create a scramble of branches. Then add leaves and flowers to further embellish your work.

There is as much root system below as Tree branching above....

couch down
Slubby yarn...
good roots
Vines & Seaweed

Musings at The edge of The Grand Canyon....
Can you imagine being a pioneer woman
all your possessions in an ox cart, The
children screaming, you're exhausted, every
bone in your body aches... You're sick of
cooking over a camp fire, your husband
Keeps Telling you "We're almost There"... and
Then you come To The edge of The grand Canyon!
Jumping would have been My first
Thought......

Turn
upside
down
and
you
have
Vines
↑
Could
be roots!

Feather Stitch. I use this stitch more than any other because it is so very versatile. The feather stitch is perfect for climbing rose bushes. If the stitcher remembers to keep alternating from single to double to triple stitches and to keep them uneven, the branching looks very realistic. Be sure to use variegated threads for a realistic look and do not be afraid to work feather stitch branches over previous stitching. This creates depth and texture. I use the feather stitch to create evergreen trees and shrubs by using three shades of greens and three layers of feather stitches. Wheat and oats can be created in the same fashion. Just remember to use shades of color to add shadow and light and to vary the threads to add depth.

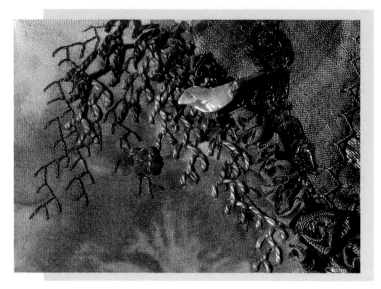

Long and Short Stitches. This versatile stitch can be used to indicate grass and weeds. If worked closely together, it can become the trunk of a tree or shrub. Just remember that light comes forward and darks recede, so use these stitches to draw with. A branch will look more rounded if you use the darker threads on the outside. Work into the center area with lighter colors. Long and short threads will create texture, either rough or shiny, depending on the threads.

Chain Stitches. The chain stitch can be used side-by-side to create trunks or branches or to act as a single outline. I often mix this with the stem stitch to give a ridged effect. Sometimes I can elongate the chain stitch into a single lazy daisy stitch to create funny little shrubs and perennial flowers. By using long and short lazy daisies and by using a variety of threads, these can be built up to give lots of depth and texture. Think of elongated lazy daisies to create saber-shaped leaves, such as the yucca cactus and the kangaroo paw plant.

French Knot. A wonderful texture can be used with French knots and variegated threads. Although it is time consuming, it is well worth the effort. I like to use these knots for old weathered branches and for trunks. French knots used in free form can indicate shrubbery on far-off hills or act as filler for the garden plants.

- SINGLE FeaTher
For deSerT shrubs
MIX Large and small
Threads! . . .

doUble FeaTher
WiTh Lazy daisy
shrub.

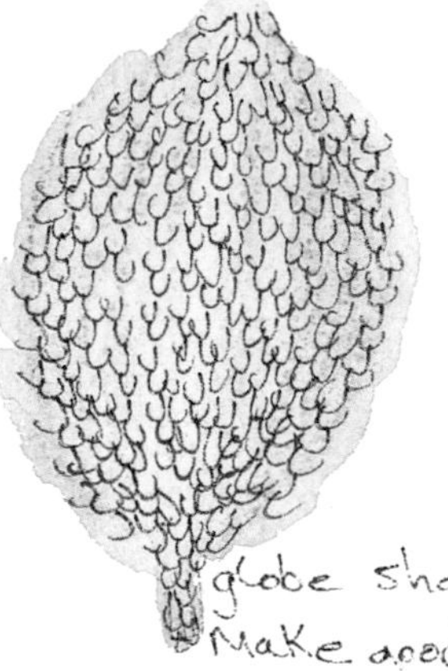

globe shapes
Make good
TUMBLEWeedS
and small
shrubs. Use
several of colour
and Threads
For More detail.

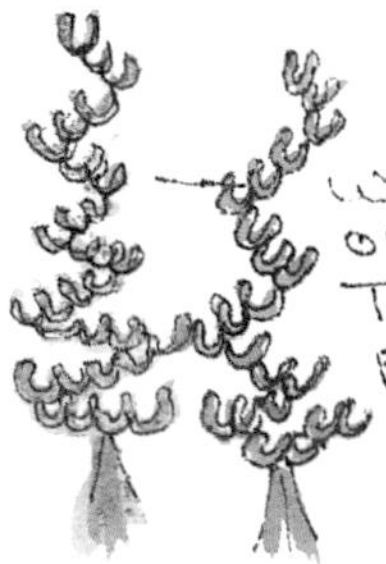

Weeds
or small shrubs.
Triple and quadruple
Feather sTitches.

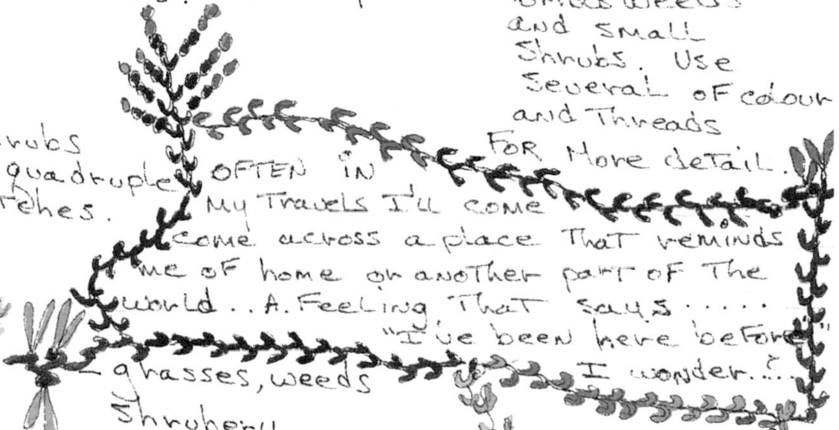

OFTEN IN
My Travels I'll come
come across a place That reminds
me of home or another part of The
world ..A.Feeling That says. . . . .
"I've been here before"
I wonder . . .

grasses, weeds
shrubery
Large FeaTher sTitch
in back
Small on Top.
Use Two shades or
Two compLimentary
colours.

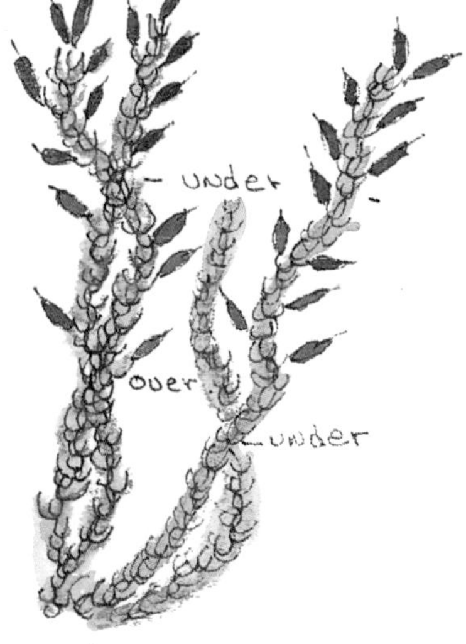

— under
— over
— under

Weeds or
TaLL plants
Use Two Layers of
FeaTher sTitch ...Two
colours - Make sure
They weave To Look
More realistic.

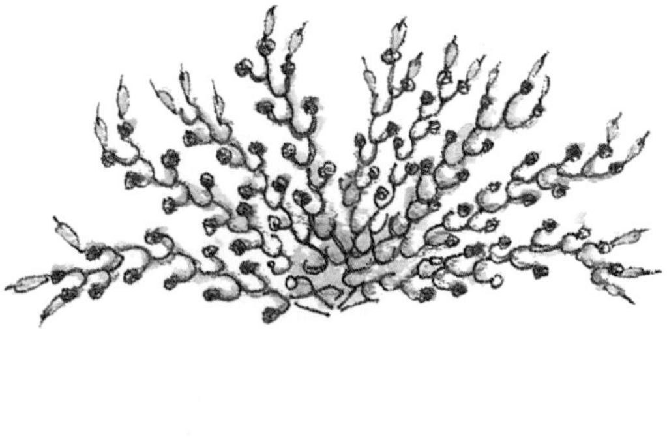

Semi circular shapes
good perrenial Flowers
good shrubs.
Add beads or Lazy daisy
STitch For Flowers.

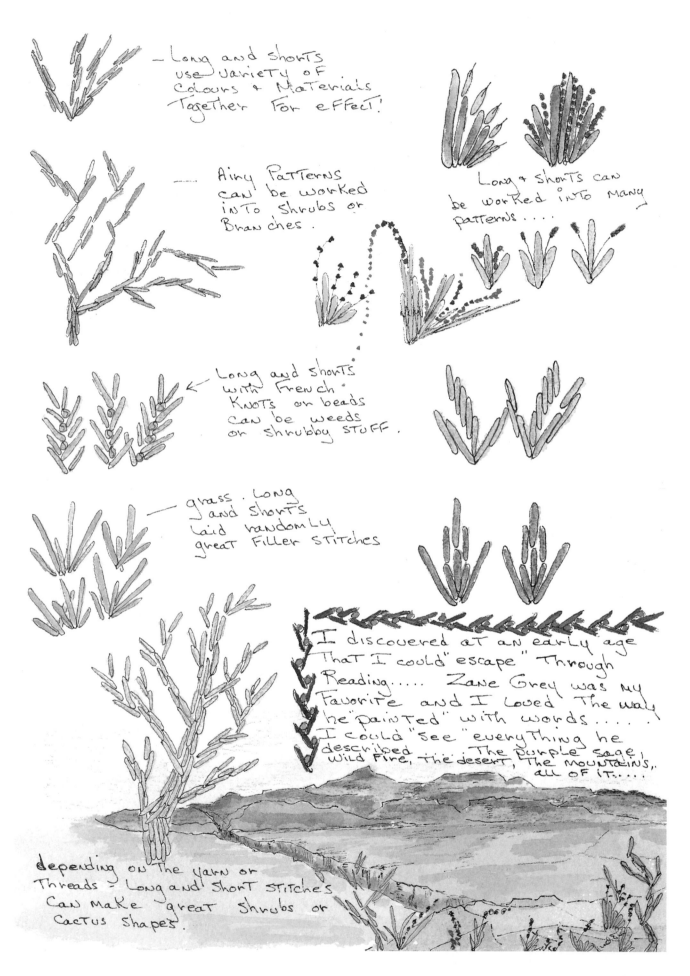

— Long and shorts
use variety of
colours & materials
together for effect!

— Airy patterns
can be worked
into shrubs or
branches.

Long & shorts can
be worked into many
patterns....

← Long and shorts
with French
Knots or beads
can be weeds
or shrubby stuff.

— grass. Long
and shorts
laid randomly,
great filler stitches

I discovered at an early age
that I could "escape" through
Reading..... Zane Grey was my
favorite and I loved the way
he "painted" with words.....
I could "see" everything he
described..... The purple sage,
wild fire, the desert, the mountains,
all of it.....

depending on the yarn or
threads - Long and short stitches
can make great shrubs or
cactus shapes.

Cottages

I have a special love for old farm houses and cottages. I suppose this has something to do with my Grandmother Shantzie's little house in High River and her beautiful big cottage garden. There is a special magic about small homes that look so cozy and lived in, polished with the patina of generations.

Grandma Baker also lived in town, but in a much larger brick house with a huge veranda across the front. This was a great place to sit and observe, skip rope, gossip, and just let the time pass by. I used this house as a reference for my story *Recollections* and there are many descriptions of it in the chapters.

I spend hours photographing, which makes for albums filled with architectural delights from Canada, Australia, Japan, Europe, and the United States. My albums are really journals of various abodes, animals, scenery, or anything that would make for an interesting painting.

More often than not, a cottage is surrounded by a garden fence, a few trees, and maybe rolling hills or mountains are in the background. Or maybe it sits on a busy street and is surrounded by other buildings. No matter where it sits, this little house has to sit either in the background, the midground, or the foreground. It is important to know the difference and to realize that the difference in size and detail is what creates perspective in your finished piece.

Unless you are standing at the corner of the cottage or looking out a window, the best place to set the cottage is in the midground where a lot of the detail can be added, and yet the foreground and the background will still highlight it. There the viewer's eye will travel directly to it.

Before I paint the cottage, I trace from a line drawing onto my fabric, using either a window or a light box. For this I use a fine line pencil, filling the sketch in later with black and brown permanent pen. If you have an old photograph and you are hesitant about sketching,

Cottages are the memories of our childhood, long lazy summer days: cat on the hearth, grandma in the garden. Cottages are what we would like to live in; but on a short term basis… especially when the winter comes!

I use a background of natural fiber, such as cotton, aida cloth, and silk, because I paint directly onto the background fabric. I will use water-based paints and dilute them down to a water-color consistency. I would much rather lay down several layers of paint than to ruin it with one heavy application. Remember that 90% of my work will never be washed in a washing machine, and a lot of it will be displayed behind glass like a painting, so I am not worried about permanence.

Brian's Cottage, *courtesy Bucilla Kit Corp.*

you can have an enlarged or reduced photocopy made of the house or cottage. Using a light box, trace the cottage on top of the fabric. Pay particular attention to where the horizon lies and sketch in a bit of the foreground. I tend to use paint instead of fabric to block in the building, because I will be using threads and yarns to create texture and design. You can use appliquéd fabrics to create the roof and the walls. (Use solid or mottled fabrics because distinct patterns are too distracting.)

If the roof is a shingled roof, woven linen would do with very fine yarn to indicate the shingle outline. A tin roof can be indicated with netting and long straight lines of threads. Always remember that the first layer of color, whether it is paint or fabric, is just the beginning. Most of the detail will be laid in with stitches of thread and yarn. Long and short stitches can be used successfully to create a thatched roof. The satin stitch will work well, too. The chain stitch laid side by side can create the look of clapboard and even act as outline details for window panes and lattice work.

Overall, as you create a cottage scene, just remember to always take a backwards journey by starting at the furthest point and by working towards the front of the picture. This will make your cottage scene more realistic and charming.

Oceans

I am fascinated by the ocean and when I was growing up, I used to fantasize about what it would look like. Being from the Alberta foothills, I did not see the ocean until I was twelve-years old. On a trip to see our great grandparents in Seattle, Washington, my sister and I went deep-sea fishing with our dad. I will never forget the overwhelming sense of total awe. How could anything be so big?

Several years ago I was on Groote Eylandt in the Gulf of Carpenteria in Australia to teach classes to the wives in the mining settlement. This beautiful, mysterious island is owned by the aboriginal people and you can visit if you are invited by their council. The beaches are made of rust to pale peach coral, and beautiful shells are everywhere. Often when walking along the beach, I would come across groups of women who had gone walk about, laughing and talking while sitting in the shade, heaps of tiny shells in their laps. The women were busily poking holes through the tough shells with a needle, preparing them for necklaces. There would always be gaggles of naked children with them who played well back from the water's edge, ever mindful that salt-water crocodiles lurked off shore.

Judith Baker Montano '93

Australian Seas

Photo: Chris Patterson

Vancouver Cove, courtesy Jason Montano

Photo: Sharon Risedorph

Cape Cod Wedding Beach,
*courtesy Jennifer Sampou
and Todd Hensley*

One morning I had been very busy gathering shells, pay-
ing particular attention to the small, brightly colored ones.
The old Blue Heeler dog who was my companion for the trip
and I got rather hot and tired, so we sat down under a
tree for some rest and shade. After a short snooze I
woke up to see a ragged line of my beautiful shells
making a mad dash for the water! Each shell was
the home of a hermit crab, and each of their little
legs was scurrying for the safety of the water. It made
me chuckle to watch them. The first to make it to safety
was a bright yellow cone shell, with a unicorn shell coming in a close second.

Seascapes are a favorite subject for me and here are a few tips that will make your work look more realistic. Know that the horizon of the water always lies perfectly flat and straight. (If you get seasick while out on the water, look at the horizon and it will calm your stomach!) Make your water fabric perfectly flat and straight. Water acts as a mirror reflection to the rocks and cliffs along the shore. This effect can be achieved with netting or tulle laid down as the reflected shape over the water. Water will also reflect the colors in the sky, whether it is a sunset or storm. Fine metallic threads in small running stitches will add shimmer to the water or shadow along the coves or inlets. Waves of water roll in over the beach sand and rocks. So when you cut out the shapes for the beach and water, always lay the water material over the beach fabric. Seagulls or other birds can be indicated with V shapes worked in fine silver metallic threads. Finally, don't forget those beautiful little shells to add in the foreground of your work.

Creative Clothing

Today, our philosophies of fashion and design are very flexible and we can live with whatever pleases us. With our easy access to all kinds of fabrics and threads, we can use wearables to show off our needlework, document a way of life, and above all, preserve our family histories and traditions. The art garment is a one-of-a-kind statement. Each and every piece is unique. Relax and enjoy this avenue of freedom. Creative clothing allows you to explore, to combine unusual fabrics and threads. As you work, your garments will take on that special feel that says "creativity!"

Children's Clothing

Decorative clothing is for everyone, including children. Use crazy quilting and needlework for decorative detail—for most people, this is the best part of garment making and the most creative.

Madeleine Montano (age 5) wearing a cotton T-dress decorated with a cross stitch design from the Vanessa Ann Collection.

Michaelá Kovacs' dress is white cotton with Chinese lace and embroidery insets (by Alison Rose for Dragonfly Company). Judith added the silk ribbon embroidery to give the dress a one-of-a-kind look.

Photo: Bill O'Connor

Joy Carlsen models a green cotton dress that has crazy quilt shoulders and an antique handkerchief bodice. The pattern is a simple T-dress made sleeveless for summer sun.

Tracy Carlsen's sundress is decorated with a crazy quilt fan. Embroidery and colorful ribbon complete the look. Andy Simpson's vest is made from a commercial pattern, decorated with a crazy quilt farm scene.

A young Madeleine Montano models a dress (upper left) embellished with crazy quilting, which shows that pastels can be used with great success. Streamers of ribbon complete the look, reminiscent of an old-fashioned English garden. The dress (upper right) was made for Madeleine's confirmation (see page 130).

Kelse Whitfield (age 2) in her birthday gift from Grandma Jude. Osh Kosh B'Gosh overalls are decorated with silk ribbon flowers around the pockets, perfect for the little gardener.

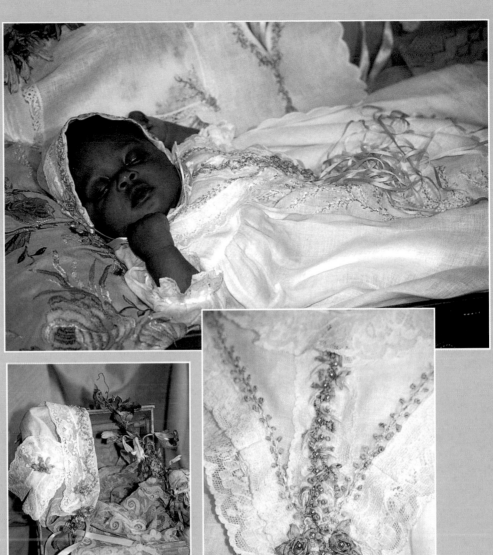

Hakeem Abdul McGinest, the youngest nephew in Judith's family, models an Irish linen christening outfit, decorated with an original silk ribbon design (courtesy G. Bird).

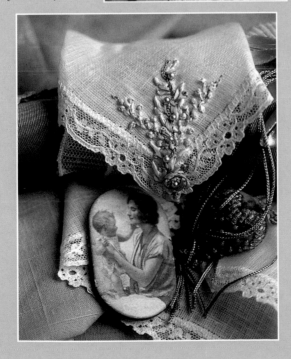

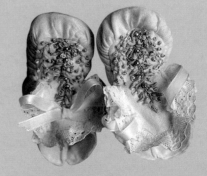

Purchased Clothing

Purchased clothing can be embellished with ease! Just choose your fabrics and embellishments carefully and decide early in the project exactly how you want it to perform. Will the garment be worn for everyday? Will you wash it? Will it be dressy or casual? How can you make the project adapt to both? How much wear and tear will it receive? Once you answer these questions, you can proceed with confidence.

Art Garments

I can't really say which came first, the turn toward individuality or my discovery of crazy quilting. I do know I was weary of ready-to-wear clothing and I wanted something different. Crazy quilting seems to be the answer. It promises gorgeous colors, asymmetrical design, and fanciful embellishments. When it beckoned with its siren song, I was ready. There was a gypsy inside me who really wanted out!

Photo: Bill O'Connor

Putting on the Ritz *was made for the Royalstar Fashion Show, presented by Fairfield Processing Corp. and Concord Fabrics. Modeled by Frances Lange.*

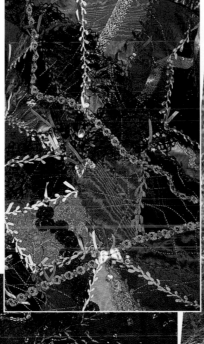

Detail of Exotic Gypsy Escapade

Photo: Bill O'Connor

Detail of Putting on the Ritz

Exotic Gypsy Escapade *was made for my daughter Madeleine and the Diamonds are a Girl's Best Friend Fashion Show, presented by Fairfield Processing Corp. and Concord Fabric. As I've watched my daughter grow, I've realized that she is the child I could never be—a free spirit, a gypsy at heart. This garment is my gift to her. Whenever she puts it on, a most magical transformation takes place. Like a living costume, this garment allows her to be who she really is. It allows her freedom of expression.*

Art-to-wear means exactly what it says—a piece of art in the form of clothing. To create art-to-wear is to release all our secret desires. Depending on the maker, art clothing can be subtle or flamboyant. For me, the joy of expressing my thoughts and feelings through crazy quilting and embellishment is a therapy all its own.

If you want a scenic crazy quilt vest, draw the scene across the front and back, and balance the design by carrying the color across both sides. Further balance is achieved by repeating stitches from side to side.

Madeleine Montano in the Indian garment Vision Quest *(detail shown on page 78). The jacket is Ultrasuede and the outfit was created for the Shining Star Fashion Show, presented by Fairfield Processing Corp. and Concord Fabrics. The eagle on the back represents the strength or vision of the Indian culture. The tree is shown firmly "rooted" in the earth of tradition.*

Photos: Bill O'Connor

Dance of the Ghosts *incorporates the deserts and mountains of the Native Americans. The desert look of soft, earth tones, spectacular sunsets, and turquoise and silver reflects a way of life as well as a region. Work the crazy quilt pieces in Indian patterns with desert colors like terra cotta, dusty pink, and sage green. Embellish the pieces with Indian fetishes or silver ornaments. Modeled by Frances Lange.*

The versatility of crazy quilting allows you to personalize a garment for your mood or lifestyle. Colors can be vibrant or subdued, fabrics can be glitzy or soft. Purchased patterns are easily adapted to crazy quilting techniques. You can make everyday street clothes and accessories, or you can design an out-of-the-ordinary garment to wear to that special art opening or dinner gala. Simple changes in color, fabric, and foundation design make crazy quilting as versatile as your imagination allows.

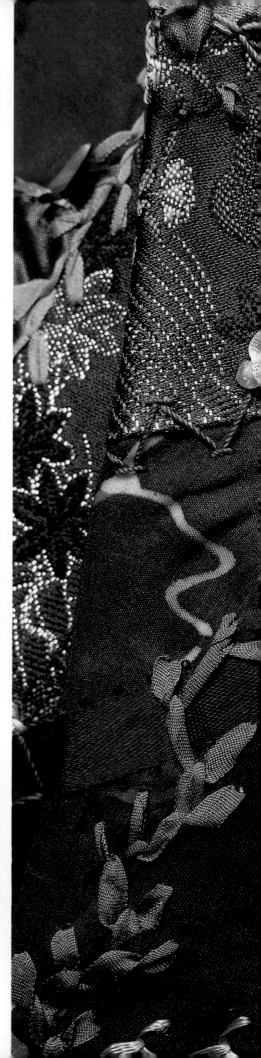

Judith and Madeleine Montano enjoy a chapter from the book Elegant Stitches, *by Judith Baker Montano.*

107

Silk ribbon can decorate everything from a favorite T-shirt dress to a vest or hat.

Art-to-wear garments are special. They can make a social or personal statement. They can be serious or just plain wild. It is quite fashionable now to mix old with new, pattern on pattern, and a whole new palette of colors. Crazy quilting and embellishment fits right in. Let your imagination guide you when you are crazy quilting.

Photo: Alan Carter

Alexandra Lober of Sydney, Australia, models her crazy quilt vest and belt made by Judith. The vest is a collection of Oriental and Australian fabrics. The antique and new laces are from England and France. The seams are embroidered with silk ribbons and highlighted with seed pearls. A spray of flowers provides a permanent corsage.

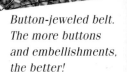

Button-jeweled belt. The more buttons and embellishments, the better!

Outfit created from a Vogue pattern. The crazy quilting is made with Japanese obi fabrics and highly decorated with silk buttonhole twist.

Photo: Bill O'Connor

110

Photo: Bill O'Connor

111

My Studio

Setting up a studio is a very personal practice, as we are all so different. Some of us like strict order and discipline, while some of us like to nest in the humble jumble of our belongings. My natural tendency is to live like a gypsy with lots of pattern, texture, and color amid the ever increasing collections of old furniture, antique collectibles, country and Motown CD's, fabric, laces, ribbons, "come to pappa" shoes, shelves of books, walls filled with art, and a cat on my lap.

Use the best materials and tools you can afford. It will pay off in the long run with better workmanship and more pride in your work.

Fortunately I have been able to add discipline to my life and I force myself to be on time, make the deadlines, and produce while on the road.

My workrooms are not large but they are well organized. Because I work with small items, such as silk ribbon, buttons, and beads, I force myself to file them away in a marked plastic bin or drawer, and I make sure to put them back when I am through—this is the hardest part of all!

My workrooms both have floor to ceiling shelving that holds clear boxes, small trays, and storage items found at the hardware store and fishing tackle shops. My fabrics are always folded, and stacked by color, type, and use. All the laces I keep in clear boxes and I divide these by type and weight. My threads and ribbons are kept on large spools and these rest on spindles so I can see them. All my tools, such as scissors, rulers, template plastic, and a rotary cutter, hang on hooks on one wall. My books and research files are kept on open shelves.

Photography is a great love in my life and I make room for it in my workroom. All my negatives, slides, and

Photo: Bill O'Connor

SETTING UP A WORKROOM

Workrooms come in all sizes but they are very necessary... I don't care if it is the size of a broom closet, you must have a space to call your own, a place to set up your supplies, and a place to leave your work unbothered. Over the years, I became an expert at setting up in the kitchen, the dining room, or where ever, but the minute I carved out a special space just for me, my work improved and I took it more seriously and so did my family.

Setting time aside for your projects is the most difficult. We wear many hats as women and we can handle more than one thing at a time. But many of us forget to take time for ourselves, let alone our needlework or projects. Because I am on the road 180 days of the year, I find myself working on airplanes, in hotel rooms, or snatching a few minutes in a moving car. For every minute of glory, I have spent hours in a dingy old track suit, glued to my work table. Of course, I regret it at times... but it has always paid off for me. So if you are ever going to set aside time for your projects and for yourself, it will take discipline and the ability to stay focused. Just remember, having organized materials and a workroom will make it easier for you!

transparencies are in file sleeves and I mark the good ones. On hand is a light table and a good loupe. I also keep a history of my work with photographs and slides filed by years. My work also consists of a huge collection of old photographs, postcards, memorabilia, and laces that will be used in my photo collages. I go out of my way to categorize all this material, storing it in photo boxes on the shelves.

Judith embroiders her wedding dress while on the road.

The only time I dig in my heels and revolt is when I am on the road. I pull all the materials for my projects, store them in fishing tackle bags and let them mix willy nilly. But after a few weeks on the road, I make myself go through the supply bags, tidy up, delete some and add some more.

Lighting is most important, aside from a good variety of materials. I spend extra money and use Ott-Lite® or color corrected light. These are the types of lights dentists use in their offices because they give off true, natural color. When I travel, I also carry an Ott-Lite light for working in hotel rooms.

I like to use a large table to lay out projects. I have the table set up high so that when I sit down to the table my elbows are chest high...this forces me to sit up taller and to keep my shoulders from stooping. I set my ironing board across the room instead of next to my sewing machine, forcing me to get up and move.

Around

the World

I never dreamed that my love of fibers would allow me to travel around the world. When I was living overseas as a young woman, I was not very interested in needlework, but I realize now that I was gathering the experiences and ideas that would show up later in my artwork. In each country I was able to live among the native people and not be confined to a compound of American patriots. Because of this, I made friends all over the world and learned at a young age that although we may speak different languages, practice different religions, and our skin colors vary, inside we are all the same. Often I can close my eyes and see the various countrysides, hear the accents, smell the markets, and the restaurants. From all these memories I have gathered that we all have hopes and dreams, we all want to be happy and content, and we all want to love and be loved...sometimes I wonder why can't we get it right...why can't we all get along?

England

Long before I ever started traveling, I was in love with the idea of it. When I married at the age of twenty five, we were sent overseas and I was absolutely delighted. We were sent first to England, which was the beginning of a seven-year stint overseas in Great Britain, Germany, and Japan, with numerous short stays in over ten other countries.

While in England, I saw my first crazy quilt at the Victoria and Albert Museum. I was fascinated with the needlework and what it represented. The quilts reminded me of my Indian friends back home in Canada and of the gypsies who traveled through Aldborough, Yorkshire. The gypsies would set up camps along the backroads for the spring horse sales. Their colorful caravans were brightly painted and the harnesses of the horses were embellished with heavy brass decorations. When the camp was set up, the women would come to town to sell fortunes and handmade clothespins. I made friends with some of them and was invited to their camp for tea. I loved the smell of the campfires, and I remember the little children who hid their eyes and then peeked from behind their mother's skirts. For a short time I wasn't homesick for my beloved Alberta foothills, and I would close my eyes and pretend I was sitting with Dorothy and Webster Lefthand in their summer camp.

Photo: Chris Patterson

No proper Englishman is without a four-legged companion and I was no different. My constant companion was a small West Highland terrier known as McDougal. Because he was a typical terrier, never minding and always into trouble, we often traveled into Thirsk to the veterinary surgery owned by a lovely man. Later this veterinarian was to gain world-wide fame under the pen name of James Herriot.

I also joined a ladies sewing circle. Although there was the Junior League, I preferred the older ladies group because they had spirit and laughed more. I even took up china painting upon their insistence. One of these eccentric old dears lived two doors from me in a two hundred year old brick cottage with a long narrow garden where she kept a pack of cairn terriers. I never could come up with a final count, as they were always on the run…maybe ten or twelve. Although she was a breeder of cairn terriers, she could not bear to part with them. The dogs were her special babies. This sweet old woman even looked like her dogs. I can still see her driving by in her old clunker of a car—hair askew, little black eyes peering through the steering wheel while balls of barking, yelping fur hurled themselves from the back seat to the front seat to the dashboard and back again.

I developed my love for antiques in England, and became an avid collector of Victoriana. I became an apprentice to an antique dealer and later went into business with a Queen's Own Master Craftsman.

Japan

There is something about the Japanese culture and the people that makes me feel very much at home, and I am comfortable with the formality and the mores of Japanese life. The Japanese respect tradition, and the arts are looked upon as an honorable profession. If you reach the title of Sensei, you are looked up to and respected. Time is irrelevant when it comes to producing something of beauty. An artist will take months, even years, to finish a project, realizing that it will be viewed as an heirloom.

My first trip to Japan as an artist was due to my association with the Denver Art Museum, which was asked to set up a display through the Mitskoshi Department Store of Tokyo. I was asked to come along as a teacher, and it was the beginning of a longtime love affair.

During my first set of classes, I was introduced to the owner of the Kanagawa Silk Company. Soon I was hired to endorse their products and to teach for them twice a year. At first I stayed in a fancy five-star hotel in the Ginza area, but over the years as we became friends, I was allowed to live in a businessman's hotel in the Kuramae wholesale district. I was also allowed more freedom when they realized I would not get lost.

My relationship with Kanagawa lasted for three and a half years and through them I met my dear friend, Eva Yagino, who is an excellent interpreter and tour guide. We have worked together for many years now.

Class at Nihon Vogue; Judith with her friend and interpreter Eva Yagino (on the author's right)

Photo: Ernest Shealy

I have a special affinity for Japan, perhaps it is because my son Jason was the New Year's baby for Okinawa in 1973. This great honor has brought him good luck throughout his life.

Photo: Bill O'Connor

The timeless beauty of silk fabrics has always had a spell on me and I spend hours searching for them in special fabric shops and antique flea markets throughout Japan. I use old kimono silks, as well as obi and dollmaking fabrics in my work. I also collect Japanese artifacts and these I nestle in among my English antiques and my western memorabilia, as if it is meant to be.

One day while shopping for our daughters, Eva spied a lovely watch. I told her it was a great buy and encouraged her to purchase it. "Oh no, Montano san, if I buy this for her, even if it is exactly what she wants, she won't like it just because her mother picked it out!" We burst into laughter, because both our teenage daughters were giving us fits at the time. It was a real eye opener for me. Teenagers are the same everywhere!

I feel at home in Japan, and now that *Elegant Stitches* has been translated into Japanese by Nihon Vogue of Japan, I have built a good relationship with the owners Seto San Senior and Junior. Through their support of the quilt world, quilting has truly come of age in Japan. I am honored to be associated with them. I have also taught in the past for Takako Onoyama of Quilt House Yama, and it is through her that I have learned so much about the Japanese culture. I consider her a close friend.

Mr. Watanabe, who owns Mokuba Ribbons, has been another great supporter of my work and through his generosity I am well supplied with ribbons. I was very touched when he spoke at a party given by Nihon Vogue and thanked me personally for all the ribbon sold in America, because of *The Art of Silk Ribbon Embroidery* and my years of teaching. I admire him very much.

Most importantly, through my students, I have discovered that needlework is a universal theme understood by all women. I see students in every country, from all walks of life, come together with the common denominator of cloth, needle, and thread. I know that I am a very lucky woman to have had so many positive experiences living and working overseas.

During our stay in Japan, the Vietnam war was in full swing. When the war ended, the company my husband worked for managed to rescue their Vietnamese staff. Many of us sheltered them in our homes until they could find work in America. I remember the women most of all, because they were so tiny, so pretty, and so frightened.

Australia

Soon after *The Crazy Quilt Handbook* was published, Gloria McKinnon of Anne's Glory Box invited me to come to Australia for a teaching tour. I will never forget the heat and the long hours I spent traveling in the back of her car, but I was hooked! It was an instant love affair with Australia.

When I lived with my godparents as a young girl, I often heard stories about their experiences traveling through Australia. We almost moved to Australia in the 1960s, because my uncle truly believed that Australia and New Zealand were the last farming and ranching frontiers. My godparents fell in love with a large farm near Wagga Wagga, Victoria, and set up the papers to purchase it. However, it soon became evident that the taxation problems would make it impossible to work out. Years later, I taught in Wagga Wagga and my godparents were right. It is wonderful farmland, the countryside is beautiful, and the people are great.

Over the last ten years I have returned regularly to Australia. I have been as far north as the Gulf of Carpentaria, as far south as Tasmania, all along the eastern coast, and even inland to Alice Springs. I have sat among the aboriginal women under their houses for shade, dived the Great Barrier Reef, watched the sheep shearers and the dog trials near Wall, Victoria, flown over Kakadoo for my fiftieth birthday, singing "Happy Birthday to me" while circling Jim Jim Falls. I've made incredible dear friends and adopted a few kids. The warmth of these people and their incredible country has had a great influence on my work. My palette is much softer now, and I have learned so many new techniques that my mind is filled with unfinished landscapes and ideas.

I hope to keep returning to Australia for many years to come, and maybe if I am lucky, one of my children will settle there to live.

The Story of Ralph

I often play a prank on my friends and students by telling them about my boyfriend Ralph. For years, I have stayed with Peter and Annie Riseborough in Melbourne, Australia. They have two great kids and a dog named Ralph. Now, Ralph is this incredible big dog in a little body, and he lives behind the cutest face ever put on a dog. He is part cairn terrier and wire-haired dachshund, so he sort of resembles a terrier that has been stretched out.

Judith with students in River Lea Cottage Quilts, Adelaide, South Australia

Photo: Ernest Shealy

I met Ralph on my first visit when he was a puppy. Annie had prepared a fabulous meal and we were all sitting in the dining room. I had slipped off my high heels under the table. After the lovely meal and lots of laughter, I put on my shoes, took a step, and fell down…dear Ralph had chewed a heel off of my favorite snakeskin shoes.

The next evening Annie was working on a special porcelain doll that she wanted to enter in the Camberwall Doll Show. It was a sleeping fairy doll and she had made a beautiful wreath of dried flowers with a long veil. Upon finishing, we were sitting at the table for tea and out of the corner of my eye a blur of white streaked by…It was Ralph with the wreath in tow, flowers flying, veil ripping. These two escapades are just the tip of the iceberg, and how he ever got from puppy to dog is beyond me. All I can say is that he is one of my best friends and I truly look forward to seeing him every year. We go for long walks and he patiently waits while I shop. We spend hours in the Kew graveyard where he can roam free while I take photographs. He is rather fickle, and while I am visiting his humans, he becomes my dog, even sleeps on my bed.

My story goes like this…I have a boyfriend in Melbourne and I visit him once a year. We have a glorious reunion every time and he is so happy to see me that he kisses me all over and won't stop jumping on me. The minute I go to bed at night, he is right there beside me (by now my students are really engrossed in my story). "Would you like to see a picture of him?" I ask. Of course they are all dying of curiosity, so I show them a picture of my boyfriend Ralph…with a face like that, what isn't there to love?!!

Dear, dear Australia with each visit she captures more of my heart…. Judith

121

United States

I am very fortunate to live in the United States and yet retain my Canadian citizenship. I was educated in Colorado and California, raised a family in Texas and Colorado, and now live between California and Colorado! I've traveled throughout this vast country with my work and I've met many wonderful Americans.

Judith with class from Heartbeat Quilts, owned by Helen Weinman of Hyannis, MA.

It gives me pause for thought to remember that all my great grandparents immigrated to Canada from Oklahoma, Kansas, North Dakota, and Illinois and now I reside back in the United States.

I was very fortunate to be in on the ground floor of the quilting revival as a student and later as a teacher. Thanks to the foresight of Karey Bresenhan and the International Quilt Market, quilting is a world-wide phenomenon. I taught crazy quilting for Karey years ago in her shop and I still enjoy teaching for her at the International Quilt Festival in Houston.

I am not exactly a quilt teacher although my beginnings started in traditional quilting. Now my fiber art balances between the quilting and needlework industry. My goal is to use the best of both worlds and to blend them into collages of mixed mediums.

Judith with Todd Hensley, publisher of C&T Publishing

Canada

Of course, Canada has been a great influence in my life, and I often use my memories of Canada for inspiration. My mother and my honorary aunties are the needleworkers I know best. From my Hutterite neighbors I have collected many samplers and engagement handkerchiefs, which I will never part with because the handwork represents my friends.

I don't teach in Canada as often as I would like and my visits home do not come often enough. Sometimes I feel guilty about living away from my country, so it was a great surprise when the Canadian government bestowed the Governor General's Award of Honor on me for my work in the arts and for representing Canada. I keep the medal on my bookshelf and it constantly reminds me of how proud I am to be Canadian.

Judith with class at Olds Agricultural College, Olds, Alberta, Canada

The influence of other countries and their people on me has been enormous, and I am most grateful for this. I plan to keep on traveling until I am old and gray, and after that if I need a cane or a chair, I will still be looking for new experiences and new friends. We only have one life to live and it passes very quickly...I for one plan to cram as much as I possibly can into my one chance at life.

Celebrations

I have a beautiful family of black, brown, white and yellow; a United Nations in one family. We are a mix of Japanese, Hungarian, African American, Cherokee Indian, French, Norwegian, Mexican American, Scots, German, and English. My world is richer for all these interesting people, and I want to grow old and gray with them.

We love celebrations of any kind: weddings, birthdays, baptisms, anniversaries, graduations, holidays—any special day will do!

Photo: Dierdre Williams

Weddings

I love weddings as they are a special coming together of family and friends in the celebration of love. What better way to celebrate with beautiful flowers, decorations, fancy clothing, music, dancing, and good food?

Ernest and I have been married four times in three countries! Because of our travels it was easier to take our weddings to all our family and friends throughout the world. We were married first in Australia in the William Rickets Sanctuary; next in Alberta, Canada at the family ranch; the last two were garden weddings in Castle Rock, Colorado and Los Angeles, California.

In this way we shared our love with family and friends and could include lots of people in the wedding parties and services. Plus we got to celebrate four times!

Detail of Australian wedding dress

Los Angeles wedding party

Groom Ernest Shealy models his crazy quilt vest, made from Japanese obi and antique fabrics.

Photo: Alan Carter

Colorado wedding party

Alberta wedding party

Australian wedding party

My husband has welcomed my children as his own. My family and friends love him for himself and for making me so happy. He has embraced my life with great enthusiasm. In return, I get to be me and he still loves me.

Birthdays

If you choose to record your family's history in needlework, start by cutting and arranging the fabric in a pleasing design, taking care to show off all the sentimental pieces. Now the fun of embellishment begins. You can lavishly cover the seams with embroidered stitches as well as lace and ribbons. Zigzag silk ribbon across the piece and secure the edges with French knots and beads. Now you can carefully work family birth dates in satin stitch or pens, complete with a favorite verse atop a white cloth triangle. From the birth dates and documentation, your family history is constructed. Whatever type of crazy quilting or embroidery appeals to you, I hope needleart will give you the inspiration and ideas to create your own family heirlooms.

Maddy's Life collage made by the author for her daughter's twenty-first birthday present. The heart centerpiece was taken from Madeleine's confirmation dress (shown on page 97).

Photos: Chris Patterson

Needlework allows the creator to be a histo-rian, sentimental poet, embroiderer, painter, seamstress, and above all, artist. For the sentimental needleworker, it becomes a depository of family memorabilia—a record of births, weddings, and achievements.

Nephew Miles

Granddaughter Rie

Grandson Gen

Granddaughter Kelse

Family and Friends

*Niece Aaleyah and
Granddaughter
Nicole*

A gift made by hand is always joyfully received. I enjoy making gifts of needlework for family and friends. These gifts can range from picture frames, jewelry, to framed collages.

Niece Dana

*Judith with Gracie and
Dorothy Lefthand*

Photo: Alan Carter

Crazy quilting appears to be timeless as it evolves from the Victorian style of yesterday to the eclectic style of today. I can hardly wait to see what tomorrow will bring!

Photo: Bill O'Connor

(Below) Gift for Di Pettigrew, depicted as a
little girl (with her sister and her mother), who
resides in Warrnambool, Australia

(Above left) Gift for Sylvia Weinman, depicted at
ages 4, 30, and 83, who resides in Hyannis, MA

Madeleine and Jason Montano at ages 17 and 20

Judith at age 6 months

For my children . . .

If we were stranded at sea and I had to choose which of my children to save, I would choose to die, while trying to save them both; for I could not live with the burden of having chosen one over the other. I gave birth to each with a full heart and open arms, and I shall love them equally 'til the day I die.

Photo: Chris Patterson

Photo: Alan Carter

Ernest Shealy

Nicole with Grandpapa

Judith and Jason Montano

135

Recollections of Life

Typical of most women my age, I was taught that true happiness was to marry a good man, keep a nice house, have children, always stand behind your husband, and live life according to everyone's expectations. I was just getting the hang of all this when out of nowhere came the women's movement. Somewhere between living life according to other's expectations and bra burning, I got jammed right between the proverbial rock and a hard spot.

I have watched with great interest, and some dismay, the pendulum sweep of women's emancipation. Many of my sisters were out there to prove that anything a man could do, they could do as well or better, and to my great delight they did. They became the "wonder women" of the eighties and most of us tried to copy them. But we became so busy that we forgot about ourselves. We had jobs in the work force, children to raise, parties to give, homes to decorate, Jones' to keep up with...rush, rush, rush...proving to everyone but ourselves that

we were liberated. Years later when we hit the pinnacle of our so-called success some of us looked in the mirror and saw sad lonely eyes. We had paid a terrible price for our liberation. Success meant empty relationships, the stress of trying to keep up, divorce, time away from children, and pretending to be happy when really most of us were pretty confused.

There is an old adage "you can't have your cake and eat it too" and many of my contemporaries found that out the hard way. They wanted liberation, but with a handsome alimony, the house, the car, custody of the children, and a social life! Yet, liberation means equal responsibility, equal fiscal responsibilities, and equal workload. I am not pointing a finger of blame at anyone, because I wanted a lot of those so-called freedoms. Also, I know how desperately we needed those brave women who marched for the vote, who demanded education, who stood up against the Vietnam war, and above all the women who stood up and said, "enough is enough, we want equality!" I just got confused on the meaning of true equality.

I have come to the realization that if we want true equality we have to be willing to accept the responsibility of it. It isn't easy to give up old ideas, drilled into our beings by the words and examples set by our mothers and their mothers. But, if this is going to work for our children, my generation has to get equality sorted out. We have to learn to share the blame and we have to look at the other side of the story. If we really want equality we have to let go of the idea that someone has to take care of us.

Sometimes when I think about equality, I have to pull myself up short and remember how far we have progressed since I was a child. Doors have opened for us and some of them have been slammed in our faces, but, surprise, surprise, we've kept our foot in the door!

I would like to tell you that after my divorce, I skipped through life as a single parent with lots of fabulous relationships and that being single is the only way to go but I failed miserably at it. I got through it with lots of therapy, lots of loneliness, lots of mistakes, and I failed a lot of my lessons. I believe that we are put on this earth to learn lessons and if we don't get it right we have to keep coming back. At the age of fifty-two this makes me very nervous so I am trying extra hard to do my homework.

So how on earth does this rambling essay on women's liberation fit into a retrospect of my artwork and career? I'd like to be flip about it all but the truth is that women's liberation is a big lesson I have struggled with and it is all woven and twisted into my life's work. My life, written in book form, would read like a dime-store novel, trying to cram too many lives and experiences into one, but I am not sorry for the way my years have careened down life's path. I've worked hard to get to this point in my life and I have paid a high price for my so-called success.

I have suffered from depression for many years and it was a secret I kept to myself, all-consuming and powerful. I confessed these feelings to my doctor and she put me through a battery of testing. To my great amazement I fit into a small category of people who make up the majority of artists, musicians, writers, and actors. You see, I never looked at myself as an artist and a writer because of my low

I do not put pen to paper every day, for writing is a soulful process. First carefully chosen words and phrases must ferment in the mind, then be rolled out over the tongue and tasted. In utterance they must flow with logic and rhythm...only then do I write them down.

Maren Francis and Judith at Hooked on Books, Castle Rock, Colorado

Judith with her brother and sisters

Family Christmas in 1996

self-esteem. There it was in black and white, for my category and type of personality...I was perfectly normal! This was the big turning point in my life.

I will always react to feelings, from the very high to the very low, and it is quite a ride at times. I just have to keep remembering that these extreme feelings will pass and I am perfectly normal for my type. I have also learned that out of sadness comes a great deal of creativity!

Often I try to joke about the time I decided to shed some light on the dark side of my life and enrolled in a class for Adult Children of Alcoholics. For the first time I was with people who spoke the same language and really understood me. I liken it to opening a can of worms: they explode out and crawl everywhere and no matter how hard you try you can never get that lid back on. So you have to get fixed or you will keep repeating all those bad habits taught to you by parents who were doing the best they could.

With this little bit of knowledge, I thought I had all the answers; but in reality it was just beginning. From this shaky start I went into therapy and began to study the Light Work, which is a three-year study course of self analysis, meditation, and religion. Now, there is nothing worse than a convert to anything, and I must have been a pain in the bum to my family and friends, for which I am very sorry but do not regret. Out of all this study and painful analysis, which I liken to peeling off the layers of an onion, I am proud to report that I am just a normal human being doing the best that she can with what she has. I have learned that the difference is that we should forgive ourselves and look for the lesson. Sometimes we do really well and sometimes we mess up, sometimes we plod along and sometimes we run. Lots of times I fall flat on my face!

Up until a few years ago I used to dream about going home... buying a few acres near my beloved Bar U... building a little cabin, very simple, my very own retreat. But sometimes dreams are better kept as dreams...

One of my biggest lessons in life has been the issue of trust. Every time I turned around I got smacked with another lesson about trust until one day I just screamed "OK, I have had enough! I will take care of myself! I will learn to be more responsible! I will not take my talents for granted!" I have learned that while it is good to have trust in people, the Power Above does not want you to be an idiot!

I finally decided to trust myself and worked hard at believing that I deserved better. I stopped apologizing for my success and started feeling proud of my accomplishments. I even went so far as to work with a lawyer and my publisher to stop copycat publications of my work. Some people assumed my method of crazy quilting was the original method and didn't ask permission to use it in their work. I also had lost a substantial amount of money because I trusted one of my employees. I should have been more responsible for my earnings, learned how to do my paperwork, and made my employee earn my trust. I went to court and managed to regain some of my embezzled monies. For the first time in my life I began referring to myself as an artist and author. It felt good and I was beginning to like myself. I even noticed a change in the way people treated me, especially my peers.

When I least expected it, I met my husband, Ernest Shealy, a beautiful six foot seven, black man who loves a strong woman and thinks big legs are sexy. He admires women who can make it on their own and he has always supported women's equality. He is confident in himself and expects others to feel the same. He is a nurturer and takes pride in keeping up a beautiful home.

Ernest played professional football and then put in years with the Los Angeles Department of Public Works doing cement and road work. He is a man's man who isn't afraid of his feminine side—in fact, he is proud of it. To top it off, he supports my work and is interested in my projects. He actually enjoys my lectures and he loves to travel with me.

I am my husband's second wife. He was married for twenty-five years to a wonderful woman. She was a free-spirited hippie from a conservative white family, and he was from the ghetto of Los Angeles. His family was black and proud of it, and they all worked hard for a living. It was the seventies when they were married…the era of the freedom marches and Martin Luther King, Jr. I think they were very brave and very special. She brought along three daughters to this union and he raised them as his own.

She was diagnosed with cancer and given 16 months to live, but through Ernest's determination and love she lived for five more years. Her greatest wish was that he find another mate and be happy, stating that he was too good of a man to waste. She died at home in the warmth and love of her family… she was truly a good person.

Her daughters tell me that if their mother were alive today, we would be good friends and I love them for that. Their life-long friends think she is responsible for our meeting and that she picked me out just for him. Through her, I have inherited three wonderful daughters, three sons-in-law, and four grandchildren. They have accepted my son and daughter with open arms and I finally have the family I have always wanted.

In all this rambling, what I am trying to say is that without struggling with the women's liberation issue and learning to feel worthwhile, I would never have fit into this unusual family. This is my reward…a family filled with strong men and women all doing the best they know how.

The Brotherhood
The road was rough, the rain was cold,
and the Black Man said to the Red Man
"Hello, I am your brother."
The Red Man held out his hand and said,
"Welcome, I've been looking for you,"
and they walked arm in arm
'til they came to a White Man who cried,
"Please stop, I am your brother."
They held out their arms and held him close,
"Welcome, we've been looking for you."
Together they walked down the road
'til a Yellow Man called out,
"Wait for me, I am your brother."
"Welcome brother, we've been looking for you,"
and they all joined hands.
Soon they were a large group of Yellow,
Brown, White, Black, and Red with the
warmth of brotherhood in their hearts.
The road was smooth, the sun was warm,
and the earth smiled and said,
"Welcome, I am your Mother."

Now that my children are young adults, I enjoy an honest relationship with them. For all the guilt and regrets I have heaped upon my shoulders, I am amazed to find that they are proud of me. My son is proud that I made a successful career out of my love for fibers and needlework. He tells his peers that I am a strong woman and that is what he is looking for in a mate. My daughter uses my life as a stepping stone towards her own independence. She wants a mate with whom she can walk beside, not behind, and definitely not in front of! I am proud of them both and they live a much more honest life than I ever did. My son is a film maker, musician, song writer, and actor. I am thrilled that he has the guts to reach for his star. My daughter is an artist and studies computer graphics. She is a free spirit and the gypsy child I always wished to be but was afraid to be. She doesn't carry around that big bag of fear like so many women of my generation, and she has become a strong, interesting woman.

I watch with admiration my quiet spoken son-in-law who quit his job to be with his baby daughter for the first year. Her mother, our aero-space engineer daughter, would have lost her job if she went on leave. He is a film editor and his work is more flexible. It was hard for her to go to work every day, because she missed the baby, but this young couple truly works at equality. He can change a diaper, cook a meal, and do the laundry with the best of them. Now that the baby is older, her mother works a three-day week, and father has gone back to work. They are happy and truly share their lives with each other.

My oldest grandchild is a beautiful young girl, dark and exotic like her Hungarian father. Together her parents encourage her to pursue a career in art. In my day we had the choice of honorable professions such as

The Calling of the Crows

Think of me…
When dark clouds hang in curtains of design
  Along the far horizon
When dove gray shadows dance and weave in harmony
  With a shy and fleeting sun

When crimson red to purple hues of dawn
  Caress the mountain pines
When magic light adds shadow deep along the valleys
  The plains and timberline

When whispy ribbon streaks of white
  Hang in azure noontime skies
To create a magic springboard for the diving, gliding hawk,
  Up high beyond the rise

When the distant rolling hills of home
  Call the sun god back to rest.
When the soaring peaks beyond
  wear crystal shafts of light
    upon their rugged breast

When viewing God's canvas of the night
  Feel the soft caressing breeze upon your cheek
And smile when you hear the calling of the crow.
  "Please think of me,
    think of me,
      of me,
        …me."

teaching, secretarial work or nursing. (Artists did not enjoy a good reputation in my day.) Now here is my oldest stepdaughter who is a high school teacher by choice and jazz pianist son-in-law encouraging their daughter to follow her dreams in an art career. How I envy her that support.

My middle grandchildren are a five-year old girl and three-year old boy. Their mother is my youngest stepdaughter, who can best be described as a brilliant, free-spirited schoolteacher. Their father is a Japanese Rhodes Scholar. They live in Yokohama, Japan, and through them I have access to the Japanese culture. I watch with fascination as she struggles with the complexities of Japanese tradition and her struggle to remain independent.

My world is richer for all these interesting people and I want to grow old and gray with them. I want my son and daughter to find mates who will honor them and share their dreams. I hope for more grandchildren who do not look at color and accept everyone as equal. I believe in the words of Martin Luther King, Jr. and hope one day that our children "will not be judged by the color of their skin, but by the content of their character."

I want to joke and play cards with my beloved sister-in-law and to exchange gardening tips with her husband. I want to tag along with my brother-in-law when he goes to his volunteer job as a cuddler for AIDS babies. I want to sit for long hours with my family retelling old stories and embellishing new ones. I hope to make lots of memories for us all. I've learned that love knows no color and is wrapped around trust and respect…it feels very good.

I plan to continue my artwork for years to come, to continue teaching, and to enjoy the people I meet through my work; but I want to take time along the way to smell the roses. Life is too short and love is a gift that has to be nurtured and cherished. So that is where I am at this minute. You can be sure I'll make more mistakes, but I'll be able to pick myself up a lot easier and there will be help along the way. I often daydream about the way my life has changed and how things happen for a reason. It occurs to me that had I known all my heartaches would be rewarded and I would meet the love of my life at age fifty, perhaps I would not have whined so much. As I look back on my life, I realize I have been a most fortunate woman.

Index

Bibliography

Montano, Judith Baker. *The Art of Silk Ribbon Embroidery.* Lafayette, CA: C&T Publishing, 1993

_____. *Crazy Quilt Odyssey, Adventures in Victorian Needlework.* Lafayette, CA: C&T Publishing, 1991

_____. *The Crazy Quilt Handbook.* Lafayette, CA: C&T Publishing, 1988

_____. *Elegant Stitches.* Lafayette, CA: C&T Publishing, 1995

_____. *Recollections.* Lafayette, CA: C&T Publishing, 1993

Pickston, Margaret. *The Language of Flowers.* New York: Viking Penguin, 1987

For more information on other fine books from C&T Publishing,
write for a free catalog from:
C&T Publishing, Inc.
P.O. Box 1456
Lafayette, CA 94549
(1-800-284-1114)
www.ctpub.com